Realism and Pragmatic Epistemology

Realism
and Pragmatic
Epistemology

Nicholas Rescher

UNIVERSITY OF PITTSBURGH PRESS

Published by the University of Pittsburgh Press, Pittsburgh, PA 15260
Copyright © 2005, University of Pittsburgh Press
Manufactured in the United States of America
Printed on acid-free paper
10 9 8 7 6 5 4 3 2 1

Library of Congress Cataloging-in-Publication Data
Rescher, Nicholas.
Realism and pragmatic epistemology / Nicholas Rescher.
p. cm.
Includes bibliographical references and index.
ISBN 0-8229-4249-6 (cloth : alk. paper)
1. Knowledge, Theory of.   I. Title.
BD161.R482 2005
121—dc22
2004025525

031306-2162 P8

For Cornelius Delaney

Contents

Preface

The theme of realism puts on the agenda the issue of the nature and extent of real existence. Perhaps the most absurd ontological position is the radical across-the-board *nihilism* of the doctrine, "Nothing whatsoever exists at all." This is far more radical than a *solipsism* holding that all that there is is oneself and one's thoughts, affects, et cetera. Now, it is sometimes said that the radical skepticism of a doctrine whose position is "We never know anything for sure" is self-defeating because of the problem that ensues when this claim is taken to fall into its own scope. However, a radical existential nihilism to the effect that "No existence claim is ever true" is *not* self-refuting (whatever else its flaws may be). For it does not fall into its own scope, since it is not an existence claim but the *denial* of one, that is, "There exists no existence claim that is true." But, of course, the fact that such a radical nihilism is not self-contradictory does not preclude its being absurd on other grounds. The prospect and purport of those other grounds provide one of the central topics in a study of realism.

Realism relates to reality, to existence, to what there is. Generically, it is the doctrine that existence claims regarding some category of items are, at least sometimes, true and, moreover, true independently of what humans (or finite intelligent beings at large) may *think* about the matter and what conventions they may adopt. Of course, what a given sentence—a particular assemblage of words and symbols of some language or other—will *mean* (what it happens to claim) is always conventional. But once the meaning is fixed, the truth of what is said need not or may possibly not be subject to *further* conventions.

With "realism" at large, so understood, there will clearly be a vast variety of particular versions. Some examples are

Number realism: "There are primes between 5 and 11."

Language realism: "There are (meaningful) statements (in English sentences) about cats"; "There are (meaningful) questions to be asked about cats."

Physical-object realism: "There are cats (in the real 'external' world)."

Psychic realism: "There are thoughts (worries, fears) about cats."

Affect realism: "There are aches, pains, mirages (as psychic processes)."

Possibility realism: "There is a possibility for cats to sit on mats."

An observation: Even if we were merely brains in vats, then, nevertheless, none of these modes of realism would be ruled out. Not even physical realism, seeing that brains and vats are physical objects!

Every mode of realism admits of two sorts of realism-denying (anti-realistic) positions, namely, the *agnostic* (skeptical) and the *negativistic* (nihilistic) version. Thus, consider number realism:

Agnostic denial: "There may well be numbers (numbers may well exist), but we do not *know* it." (Skepticism)

Negativistic denial: "There just are no numbers: Numbers do not exist." (Nihilism)

The long and short of it is that most realism-denying positions are highly problematic if not actually absurd, including those of all versions of the doctrine considered above, with the possible exception of denial of physical object realism, which could succumb to the radical skepticism of a Cartesian deceiver hypothesis.

This book addresses such fundamental issues in ontology from the angle of ideas and concepts of philosophical pragmatism. Its deliberations cover such topics as the theoretical basis for our knowledge claims regarding the world's facts and its lawful order, how we are to think cogently about matters of fact as contrasted with mere possibility, and how we can manage our cognitive affairs sensibly in situations of imperfect information. The realms of fact and mere possibility thus both fall within the book's pragmatic purview. Throughout, it endeavors to show how the pragmatic and purposive setting of our putative knowledge of the real world proves to be crucial not only for the processual constituting but also for the resulting constitution of our knowledge.

Accordingly, the chapters of the book, though addressing different issues, comprise a unity of topic and theme. They combine to convey the instructive message that our functional and purposive concerns exert a significant formative influence on the conduct of rational inquiry and on the way we can and should regard its products. The salient lesson of the book's deliberations are this, that while the inherent difficulties of a reality-rejecting antirealism render this position markedly unattractive, the challenging question nevertheless remains of just what sort of realism is going to be viable. Some of the key challenges of the topic lie with just this issue.

I am grateful to Estelle Burris for her help in preparing the manuscript for publication.

Realism and Pragmatic Epistemology

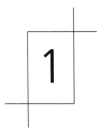

Personal Experience and Realistic Ontology

There Is No Logically Compelling Transit from Personal Experience to Objective Fact

Immediate experience is the doorway through which we obtain information about the world and our place in it. But this totally plausible contention poses the big problem of how we are to get from here to there. How can immediate experience, always personal and subjective, manage to inform us about matters of impersonal fact regarding objective reality? Interestingly enough, the answer to this impressively theoretical question has a deeply pragmatic cast.

First, a word about experience. Immediate experience comes in many forms: *external sense experience* (seeing, hearing, smelling), *inwardly sensuous experience* (pain, seasickness, hunger), *affective experience* (fear, elation), *cognitive experience* (puzzlement, interest), *aesthetic experience, religious experience,* among others. What will mainly concern us here is the first of these—in particular, the relation between people's own perceptions and the objective arrangements regarding which they are generally supposed to inform us.

Experience, to reemphasize, is as such inevitably personal and subjective. It is invariably somebody's experience, always owned by and personal to some individual. At the level of immediacy there is no such thing as impersonal experience; experience has an ineliminably biographical character.

Of course, people's experiences can agree. And when this happens we can move from *I* to *we:* "We take ourselves to be looking at a dog"; "We are all under the impression that the pavement is wet"; and so on. The experiences of individuals need not be discordant: they can manage to be accordant—and often are. But accordant or not, they remain what they are: the inevitably personal experiences of particular individuals. Experiences that agree are still just so many personal experiences that happen to be in accord. Consensus is not yet objectivity.

There is thus an inevitable gap between perceptual—and thereby personal—experience and objective fact. Contentions on the order of "It appears to me/us that there is a cat on the mat" or "I/we take myself/ourselves to be looking at a cat on the mat" are always about ourselves and will inevitably fall short of stating an objective fact such as "There (actually) is a cat on the mat." For appearing does not guarantee being. The natural reaction to a claim like "I take myself to be seeing a cat on the mat" or "I am having a cat-on-the-mat seeing experience" is "You sound like an interesting person; tell me more about yourself." Be they idiosyncratic or consensual, personal or shared, all such experience-detailing statements will, strictly speaking, be about the experiencing individuals at issue and not about the real world as such. The reports of experience are invariably autobiographical.

There is, accordingly, an unavoidable evidential gap between statements regarding the experience of people (oneself included!) and those that concern the world's objective and impersonal arrangements. The very meaning of objective factual statements is such that no volume of claims in the language of experience can stand equivalent to reality-geared theses of objective fact. If objective information about the world's arrangements is what we are after in inquiry, then immediate experience in and by itself cannot take us there. And it is instructive to consider the reason why.

Objective Reality Outruns Experience

To begin with, it is clear that, as we standardly think about things within the conceptual framework of our fact-oriented thought and discourse, any object in the real world has more facets than it will ever actually manifest in experience. For every objective property of a real thing has consequences of a dispositional character and these are never completely surveyable because the dispositions that particular concrete things inevitably have endow them with an infinitistic aspect that cannot be comprehended within experience.[1] This desk, for example, has a limitless manifold of phenomenal features of the type: "having a certain appearance from a particular point of view." It is perfectly clear that most of these features will never be actualized in experience. Moreover, a thing effectively is what it does: entity and lawfulness are coordinated correlates—a good Kantian point. And this fact, that real things involve lawful comportment, means that the finitude of experience precludes any prospect of the exhaustive manifestation of the descriptive facets of any real things.[2]

Physical things in particular have not only more properties than they will ever actually manifest but also more than they can possibly manifest. This is so because the dispositional properties of things always involve what might be characterized as mutually preemptive conditions of realization. A cube of sugar, for example, has the dispositional property of reacting in a particular way if subjected to a temperature of 10,000 degrees Celsius and of reacting in a certain way if emplaced for one hundred hours in a large, turbulent body of water. But if either of these conditions is ever realized, it will destroy the lump of sugar as a lump of sugar and thus block the prospect of the other property's being manifested. The perfectly possible realization of various dispositions may fail to be mutually composible, and so the dispositional properties of a thing cannot ever be manifested completely—not just in practice but also in principle. Our objective claims about real things always commit us to more than we can ever actually determine about them.

The existence of this latent (hidden, occult) sector is a crucial feature of our conception of a real thing. Neither in fact nor in thought can we ever simply put it away. To say that an apple possesses only those features it actually manifests is to run afoul of our conception of an apple. To deny—or even merely to refuse to be committed to the claim—that the apple would manifest particular features if certain conditions came about (for example, that it would have such-and-such a taste if eaten) is to be driven to withdrawing the claim that it is an apple. The process (corroborating the implicit contents of our objective factual claims about something real) is potentially endless, and such judgments are the "nonterminating" in C. I. Lewis's sense.[3] This cognitive depth of objective factual claims—inherent in the fact that their content will always outrun the evidence for making them—means that their endorsement always involves some element of evidence-transcending conjecture.

That my immediate experience bears upon and relates to an authentically real item that lies objectively outside the experiential domain—that it authorizes me to make claims about such an experience-transcendent reality—is accordingly something I cannot establish solely on the basis of considerations invoking such experiences themselves. The very concepts at issue (namely, "experience" and "manifestation") are such that we can only ever experience those features of a real thing that it actually manifests. But the preceding considerations show that real things do and must always have more experientially manifestable properties than they can ever actually manifest in experience. The experienced portion of a thing is similar to the part of the iceberg that shows above the water's surface. All real things are necessarily thought of as having hidden depths that extend beyond the limits, not only of experience but also of experientiability. To say of something that it is an apple or a stone or a tree is to become committed to claims about it that go beyond the data we have—and even beyond those that we can, in the nature of things, ever actually acquire. The "meaning" inherent in the assertoric commitments of our factual statements is never exhausted by their verification. Real things are cognitively opaque; we cannot see to the bottom of them; our knowledge about them can thus become more extensive without thereby becoming more complete. The idiosyncratic detail of the real outruns the reach of experientially based information.

Interpersonal Discourse Demands Objectivity

This situation is not particularly good news, for the fact is that we cannot achieve interpersonal communication without achieving an objectivity that goes beyond the limits of our experience. Agreement and disagreement about common objects of concern require impersonal objectivity. Where we do not focus on a common object whose status and standing are independent of our own experiential stance no agreement or disagreement is possible. If you say "I take myself to be seeing a cat on a green mat and it looks brown to me" while I say "I take myself to be seeing a cat on a green mat by a stone fireplace and it looks white to me" we neither agree nor disagree—our statements deal with disjointed issues: your subjective experience and mine, respectively. Contentions about distinct items cannot be brought into coordination—be it by way of agreement or disagreement. What is needed to achieve this communicatively essential desideratum is a commonality of focus through an objectivistic realism that altogether transcends the resources of immediate experience. But given the limited bearing of immediate experience, can such a realism lay claim to rational warrant? Does it actually have a sensible rationale?

Realism Roots in Ignorance, Not in Knowledge

How are we to arrive at objective statements about the real world? Surely science affords our best option here. Yet even though the science of the day affords our *best* estimate of the truth of things, it is still bound to be an *imperfect* estimate. It does not take much knowledge of the history of science to realize that science can really go wrong and steadily undergoes a process of ongoing revision. Surely the scientists of the year 3000 will think no better of our science than we think of the science of three hundred years ago. And this, too, has an important bearing on our problem of objectivity and realism.

What is perhaps the most effective impetus to realism lies in the limitations of human intellect, pivoting on the circumstances that we realize full well that our putative knowledge does *not* do full justice to the real truth of what reality is actually like. This, surely, is one of the best arguments for a realism that turns on the basic idea that there is more to reality than we humans do or can know. Traditional scientific realists see the basis for realism in the substantive knowledge of the sciences; the present metaphysical realism, by contrast, sees its basis in our realization of the inevitable *shortcomings* of our knowledge—scientific knowledge included.

Such a position automatically preempts the preceding sort of objection. For if we are mistaken about the reach of our cognitive powers—and thereby forced to acknowledge that they do not adequately grasp "the way things really are"—then this very circumstance clearly *bolsters* the case for the sort of realism now at issue. The cognitive intractability of things is something about which, in principle, we cannot delude ourselves altogether, since such delusion would illustrate rather than abrogate the fact of a reality independent of ourselves. The virtually inevitable imperfection of our knowledge is one of the most salient tokens there is of a reality out there that lies beyond the inadequate gropings of mind.

The fact of it is that a meaningful realism can only exist in a state of tension. For the only reality worth having is one that is in some degree knowable. And so it is the very limitation of our knowledge—our recognition that there is more to reality than what we do and can know or ever conjecture about it—that speaks for the mind-independence of the real. It is important to stress against the skeptic that the human mind is sufficiently well attuned to reality that *some* knowledge of it is possible. But it is no less important to join with realists in stressing the independent character of reality, acknowledging that reality has a depth and complexity of makeup that outruns the reach of mind.

We thus reach an important conjuncture of ideas. The ontological independence of things—their transcendence of the deliverances of perception and their autonomy of the machinations of mind—is a crucial aspect of realism. And the fact that this lies at the very core of our conception of a real thing, that such items project beyond our cognitive reach, betokens a conceptual scheme fundamentally committed to objectivity. The only plausible sort of ontology is one that contemplates a realm of reality that outruns the range of knowledge (and, indeed, even of language), adopting the stance that character goes beyond the limits of characterization. It is a salient aspect of the mind-independent status of the objectively real that the features of something real always transcend what we know about it. Indeed, yet further or different facts concerning a real thing can always come to light, and all that we *do* say about it does not exhaust all that *can and should* be said about it. Objectivity and its concomitant commitment to a reality beyond our subjective knowledge of it are thus fundamental features of our view of our own position in the world's scheme of things. It is the very limitation of our knowledge of things—our amply evidentiated recognition that reality extends beyond the horizons of what we can possibly know or even conjecture about it—that betokens the mind-independence of the real.

Objectivity and Postulation

The fact is that we do and should always think of real things as having hidden depths inaccessible to us finite knowers—that they are always cognitively opaque to us to some extent. And this has important ramifications that reach to the very heart of the theory of communication.

Any particular thing—the moon, for example—is such that two related but critically different versions can be contemplated:

1. the moon, the actual moon as it "really" is; and
2. the moon as somebody (you or I or the Babylonians) conceives of it.

The crucial fact to note in this connection is that it is virtually always the first version that we *intend* to communicate or think (self-communicate) about—the thing *as it is,* not the thing *as somebody conceives of it* on the basis of experience. Yet we cannot but recognize the justice of Kant's teaching that the "I think" (I maintain, assert) is an ever-present implicit accompaniment of every claim or contention that we make. This factor of attributability dogs our every assertion and opens up the unavoidable prospect of "getting it wrong."

Communication requires not only common *concepts* but common *topics,* shared items of discussion. However, this fundamental objectivity intent—the determination to discuss "the moon itself" (the real moon) regardless of how untenable one's own *ideas* about it may eventually prove to be—is a basic precondition of the very possibility of communication. If my statements dealt with *my* moon and yours with *yours,* then neither agreement nor disagreement would be possible. We are able to say something about the (real) moon thanks to our subscription to a fundamental communicative convention or "social contract" to the effect that we *intend* ("mean") to talk about it, the very thing itself as it "really" is, our own private conception or misconception of it notwithstanding. When I speak about the moon, even though I do so on the basis of my own conception of what is involved here, I will nevertheless be taken to be discussing "the *real* moon" by virtue of the basic conventionalized intention at issue with regard to the operation of referring terms.

Any pretentions to the predominance, let alone the correctness, of our own potentially idiosyncratic experience-based conceptions about things must be put aside in the context of communication. The fundamental intention to deal with the objective order of this "real world" is crucial. If our assertoric commitments did not transcend the information we ourselves have on hand, we would never be able to "get in touch" with others about a shared objective world. No claim is made for the *primacy* of our conceptions, or for the *correctness* of our conceptions, or even for the mere *agreement* of our conceptions with those of others. The fundamental intention to discuss "the thing itself" predominates and overrides any mere dealing with the thing as we ourselves conceive of it. In the context of communication, our own idiosyncratic experience of things gets relegated into the background.

Our discourse *reflects* our experience-coordinated conceptions of things and perhaps *conveys* them, but it is not in general substantively *about* them but rather about the objective and impersonal affairs upon which they actually or putatively bear.

Ontology as a Work of Conception: On Experience in the Second (Historic, Immediate, Nonaffective) Sense

A glance at any philosophical dictionary suffices to show that ontology constitutes philosophy's endeavor to resolve fundamental questions about the status and nature of reality. From the very outset there are two fundamental issues here:

1. What entitles us to claim *that* there is such a thing as mind-independent reality?
2. What can we justifiably say regarding *what* that reality is like?

The first of these issues comes down to the question of what entitles us to claim that subjective experience constitutes evidence for the existence of an extra-experiential objective order. And this, as we have just argued, is a matter of postulation—of a stipulative commitment that is ultimately retrojustified ex post facto through functional efficacy, through the useful and productive consequences for which it provides. "Just go forward on this basis, and confidence in its prosperity will emerge in due course."

On the other hand, the second issue is ultimately resolved by means of an inference to the optimal systematization. That is, if you want to know what natural reality is really like, then the best estimate available to us lies in the teachings of the actual science of the day. What experience rather than theoretical reflection shows is that if one seeks to know what natural reality is like—its composition and modus operandi—then natural science offers our best available route. That our best is no more than an imperfect estimate is itself, of course, one of the salient object lessons of the history of science. But significant though it doubtless is, it is and remains our best available estimate. And here, as elsewhere, no more can reasonably be asked of us than to do the very best that we can actually manage in the prevailing circumstances.

The Functionalistic Rationale of Realism

Reality (on the traditional metaphysicians' construction of the concept) is the condition of things answering to "the real truth"; it is the realm of what really is as it really is. The pivotal contrast is between "mere appearance" and "reality as such," between "our picture of reality" and "reality itself," between what actually is and what we merely think (believe, suppose) to be. And our allegiance to the conception of reality, and to this contrast that pivots upon it, is rooted in an acknowledgement of fallibilism.

Our commitment to the mind-independent reality of "the real world" stands coordinate with our acknowledgment that, in principle, any or all of our *present* ideas as to how things work in the world, at *any* present, may well prove to be untenable. Our conviction in a reality extending well beyond our imperfect understanding of it roots in our sense of the imperfections of our scientific world picture—its tentativity and potential fallibility. In abandoning our commitment to a mind-independent reality, we would lose our hold on the very concept of inquiry.

For one thing, we desperately need the conception of reality in order to operate the causal model of inquiry about the real world. Our standard picture of man's place in the scheme of things is predicated on the fundamental idea that there is a real world (however imperfectly our inquiry may characterize it) whose causal operations produce *inter alia* causal impacts upon us, providing the basis of our world picture. Reality is viewed as the causal source and basis of the appearances, the originator and determiner of the phenomena of our cognitively relevant experience. "The real world" is seen as causally operative in providing for the thought-external shaping of our thought and thereby in providing an underlying basis for the adequacy of our theorizing.

After all, the conception of a mind-independent reality accordingly constitutes a central and indispensable element in our thinking. For it is seen as the target and *telos* of the truth-estimation process at issue in inquiry, providing for a common focus in communication and communal inquiry. The "real world" thus constitutes the "object" of our cognitive endeavors in both senses of this term—the *objective* at which they are directed and the *purpose* for which they are exerted. And reality is seen as pivotal here, affording the existential matrix in which we move and have our being, and whose impact upon us is the prime mover for our cognitive efforts. All of these facets of the concept of reality are integrated and unified in the classical doctrine of truth as it corresponds to fact (*adaequatio ad rem*), a doctrine that only makes sense in the setting of a commitment to mind-independent reality.

Accordingly, the justification for this fundamental presupposition of objectivity and realism is not *evidential* at all, seeing that postulates are not based on evidence. Rather, it is *functional.* For we need this postulate to operate our conceptual scheme. The justification of this postulate accordingly lies in its utility. We could not form our existing conceptions of truth, fact, and inquiry without a precommitment to the independent reality of an external world. In the absence of this presupposition, we simply could not think of experience and inquiry as we do.

The Pragmatic Dimension

The ontological thesis that there is a mind-independent physical reality to which our inquiries address themselves more or less adequately—and no doubt always imperfectly—is the key contention of realism. But on the telling of the presenting analysis, this basic thesis has the epistemic status of a presuppositional postulate that is validated in the first instance by its functional utility and ultimately retrovalidated by the satisfactory results of its implementation (in both practical and theoretical respects). Without a presuppositional commitment to objectivity—with its acceptance of a real world independent of ourselves that we share in common—inquiry into and interpersonal communication about a shared, objective world would become impracticable.

Realism, then, is not a factual discovery but a functional postulate justified, in the first instance at any rate, by its practical utility or serviceability in the context of our aims and purposes, seeing that if we did not *take* our experience to serve as an indication of facts about an objective order we would not be able to validate any objective claims whatsoever.

From this prospective, too, we see once again that realism is a position to which we are constrained not by the push of evidence but by the pull of purpose. At bottom, a commitment to realism is an *input* into our investigation of nature rather than an *output* thereof. At bottom, it does not represent a discovered fact but a methodological presupposition of our praxis of inquiry; its status is not constitutive (fact-descriptive) but regulative (praxis-facilitating).

Now insofar as ontological realism ultimately rests on such a pragmatic basis, it is not based on considerations of independent substantiating evidence about how things actually stand in the world but rather on considering, as a matter of practical reasoning, how we do (and must) think ontologically about the world within the context of the projects to which we stand committed. This, to be sure, is only the starting point. Having made such a start, what we can—and do—ultimately discover is that by taking this realistic stance we are able to develop a praxis of inquiry and communication that proves effective in the conduct of our affairs. What experience can teach us is that matters run swimmingly once we initially embark on this postulation— that essential human enterprises such as inquiry and communication work out in an efficient and effective way when we proceed on this basis. And so ultimately pragmatic efficacy comes along to satisfy the demands of pragmatic utility.

After all, it makes no sense to try to compare our *putative* truth with the *real* truth, since when something does not represent our *best-available estimate* of the real truth it just would not be our *putative* truth. And so the best-available and most realistically practicable check that we do and can have that our truth-estimates are in order is that their deliverances work out in applicative practice, or rather, more systematically, that the processes and procedures by which they are established are better qualifying than the available alternatives at systematically providing propositions that prove themselves effective in this way.[4]

To be sure, this pragmatic impetus is also based on "experience"— but now in a rather different sense of the term. After all, the term *experience* is very equivocal in English. It can mean:

- Immediate perceptive experience via the internal or external senses (seeing, hearing, feeling queasy, being hungry); German: *Empfindung.*
- Personal participation in an eventuation of some sort (an earthquake, a muting, a famine); German: *Erlebnis.*
- A complex or general course of events in which one participates—as in "experience teaches," "the experience of many years indicates," "a long course of experience shows"; German: *Erfahrung.*

Now, the sense of the term operative here is not that of immediate experience (*Empfindung*) but of experience in the variant, systematic sense of *Erfahrung*—of a course of historical experience that involves a communal trial and error amidst the vicissitudes of world history's complex manifold of contingent and often fortuitous occurrences. Thus, what is pivotal for ontology in light of this discussion is not immediate experience but historical experience in its larger transtemporal and transpersonal sense of the term. Ontology is a matter of *conception* rather than *perception*. Perceptive interaction with the word is of course a necessary condition for securing information about it by a finite intelligence. And so to effect a transition from "experience" to ontology we have to recognize that *immediate* experience is no more than a starting point. Only experience in the larger, collective and historical sense of the term at issue with *Erfahrung* can provide the more powerful instrumentality required for a cognitive transit from the realm of experiential phenomenology into that of a realistic ontology.

The Issue of Validation

The grounding of our factual claims—their entitlement to be seen as cogent and correct—accordingly roots in pragmatic considerations. For there indeed is good rational warrant for our accepting these various potentially fallible factual claims as true. Two lines of consideration come into play here. The first is need—that we are creatures who require information to guide our actions in the world. But the paramount consideration involves the perspective of realism, now not in the metaphysical sense of the term but in the attitudinal sense of confining one's expectations "realistically" within the limits of the achievable. This comes into play in the present context through the consideration that the sort of truth estimation afforded by the standard epistemic norms is the best that can be done in the circumstances given the resources at our disposal. The following chapters will develop this pragmatic story in greater detail and will exhibit its bearing on our knowledge of reality in a wide variety of cognitive contexts.

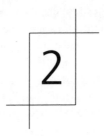

2

Realism in Pragmatic Perspective

The Existential Component of Realism

Realism has two indispensable and inseparable components—the one existential and ontological, the other cognitive and epistemic. The former maintains that there indeed is a real world—a realm of concrete, mind-independent, objective reality. The latter maintains that we can to some extent secure adequate descriptive information about this mind-independent realm—that we can validate plausible claims about some of the specifics of its constitution. This second contention obviously presupposes the first, seeing that behind the question "Are our claims about an item correct?" there unavoidably stands the question "Is there indeed such an item for our claims to be about?" But how can that pivotal, ontological thesis of metaphysical realism be secured within a generally pragmatic approach? How can functional considerations of use and purpose come to have a relevant, let alone *formative*, bearing on theoretical matters of correctness, truth, and fact?

The answer here lies in the consideration that metaphysical realism represents a commitment that we *presuppose* for our inquiries rather than *discover* as a result of them. For we do not—cannot—discover as a result of (mind-managed!) inquiry and investigation that a totally mind-detached reality actually exists. This is clearly not an inductive inference issuing from the scientific systematization of our observations but rather represents a regulative, thought-guiding presupposition that makes empirical inquiry possible in the first place. How could we possibly learn from observation that our mental experience is itself largely the causal product of the machinations of a mind-independent manifold—that subjective experience has objective bearing because all those phenomenal appearances are causally rooted in an altogether mind-external physical realm whose reach and range outrun the confines of our experience?

What is ultimately at issue here is a practice-enabling presupposition that experience is indeed objective. That what we *take* to be evidence indeed *is* evidence, that our sensations yield information about an order of physical existence outside the experiential realm itself, and that this experience is not just merely phenomenal but represents the appearance of something extra-mental belonging to an objectively self-subsisting order—all this is something that we must always *presuppose* in using experiential data as "evidence" for how things stand in the world. For if we did not presume from the very outset that our sensations somehow relate to an extra-mental reality so as to be able to evidentiate claims about its nature, then we could clearly make no use of them to draw any inference whatever about "the real world."

Commitment to a mind-independent reality is, all too clearly, a *precondition for* empirical inquiry rather than a *consequence of* it—a presupposition we have to make to be able to use observational data as sources of objective information. We really have no alternative but to *presume or postulate* it. Objectivity represents a postulation made on *functional* (rather than *evidential*) grounds: we endorse it in order to be in a position to learn by experience. What is at issue here is not so much a product of our experience of reality as a factor that makes it possible to view our experience as being "of reality" at all. As Kant clearly saw, objective experience is possible only if the existence of such a real, objective world is an available given from the outset rather than the product of experience—an *ex post facto* discovery about the nature of things.[1]

Our endorsement of the reality of observation-engendering causes in nature—which as *causes of experience* in the order of being also do double duty as inferences there from in the order of learning—is not based on empirical investigation but on general principles of a procedural character. What we learn from science is not and cannot be *that* an inherently unobservable sub-observable order of physical causality undergirds nature as we observe it, but rather *what*—with their reality taken as given—these underlying and preliminarily presumed agencies must specifically be like. Science does not (cannot) teach us *that* the observable order emerges from underlying unobserved causes and that the phenomena of observation are signs betokening this extra- and subphenomenal order of existence. For this is something that we must presume from the outset of any world in which *observation* as we understand it can transpire. What science does teach us (and metaphysics cannot) is what can plausibly take to be the descriptive character of this phenomena-engendering order once its existence is taken for granted. For once an objective reality and its concomitant causal operation has been postulated, then principles of inductive systematization, of explanatory economy, and of common cause consilience can work wonders in exploiting the phenomena of experience to provide the basis for plausible claims about the nature of the real. But we indispensably need that initial existential presupposition to make a start. Without that natural commitment to a reality serving as ground and object of our experience, its cognitive import will be lost. Only on this basis can we proceed evidentially with the exploration of the interpersonally public and objective domain of a physical world-order that we share in common. Only by way of a facilitating presupposition—albeit one that is ultimately retrovalidated through its applicative utility and efficacy—can we ever hope to establish that our observational experience (unlike our dream experience) is ever *evidence* for anything objectively mind-external, that is, able to provide information about a "real world."

Accordingly, that second, descriptive (evidential) component of realism stands on a very different footing from the first, existential (presuppositional) component. For reality's *nature* is something about which we can only make warranted claims through actually examining it. Substantive information must come through inquiry, through evidential validation. Once we are willing to credit our observational data with objectivity—with reality-orientation and thus with evidential bearing—then we can, of course, make use of them to inform ourselves as to the nature of the real. But the objective bearing of observational experience is not something that we can preestablish; it is something we must presuppose in the interest of honoring Peirce's pivotal injunction never to bar the path of inquiry. And the functional nature of this practice-enabling presupposition means that the validation process at work must, at this fundamental level, be altogether pragmatic. It represents a step we take prospectively in order to put ourselves into a position to satisfy our goals.

Realism in Its Regulative/Pragmatic Aspect

The preceding deliberations point clearly in the direction of a pragmatic justification for a realistic stance toward our experience as intensionally indicative of something beyond itself. The commitment to realism is the possibilizing instrumentality for a certain practical modus operandi. Accordingly, we have good reason—good *pragmatic* reason—for standardly operating on the basis of the "presumption of objectivity" reflected in the guiding precept: "Unless you have good reason to think otherwise (that is, as long as nothing impedes: *nihil obstat*), treat the materials of inquiry and communication as veridical—as representing the nature of the real." The ideal of objective reality is the focus of a family of convenient regulative principles—a functionally useful instrumentality that enables us to transact our cognitive business in the most satisfactory and effective way. Bearing this pragmatic perspective in mind, let us consider this issue of utility and ask what this postulation of a mind-independent reality actually does for us.

The answer is straightforward. The assumption of a mind-independent reality is essential to the whole of our standard conceptual scheme relating to inquiry and communication. Without it, both the actual conduct and the rational legitimation of our communicative and investigative (evidential) practice would be destroyed. To be evidentially meaningful, experience has to be experience of something. And nothing that we do in this cognitive domain would make sense if we did not subscribe to the conception of a mind-independent reality. And since this is not a learned fact, it is—must be—an assumption whose prime recommendation is its utility.

To begin with, we indispensably require the notion of reality to operate the classical concept of truth as "agreement with reality" (*adaequatio ad rem*). Once we abandon the concept of reality, the idea that in accepting a factual claim as true we become committed to how matters actually stand—"how it really is"—would also go by the board. The very semantics of our discourse constrains a commitment to realism; we have no alternative but to regard as real those states of affairs that are affirmed by the contentions we are prepared to accept. Once we put a contention forward by way of serious assertion, we must view as real the states of affairs it purports and must see its claims as facts. We need the notion of reality to operate the conception of truth. A factual statement on the order of "There are pi mesons" is true if and only if the world is such that pi mesons exist within it. By virtue of their very nature as truths, true statements must state facts: they state what really is so, which is exactly what it means to "characterize reality." The conceptions of *truth* and *reality* come together in this notion of *adaequatio ad rem*—the venerable principle that to speak truly is to say how matters stand in reality, in that things actually are as we have said them to be.

In the second place, the nihilistic denial that there is such a thing as an objectively mind-independent realm would destroy once and for all the crucial Parmenidean divide between appearance and reality. And this would exact a fearful price from us, since we would then be reduced to talking only of what we (I, you, many of us) *think* to be so. The crucial contrast notion of the *real* truth would no longer be available: we would only be able to contrast our *putative* truths with those of others but could no longer operate the classical distinction between the putative and the actual, between what people merely *think* to be so and what actually *is* so. We could not take the stance that, as the Aristotelian commentator Themistius put it, "that which exists does not conform to various opinions, but rather the correct opinions conform to that which exists."[2]

The third point relates to the issue of cognitive coordination. Communication and inquiry, as we actually carry them out, are predicated on the fundamental idea of a real world of objective things, existing and functioning "in themselves," without specific dependence on us and so equally accessible to others. Intersubjectively valid communication can only be based on common access to an objective order of things. All our ventures at communication and communal inquiry are predicated on the stance that we communally inhabit a shared world of things. They presuppose there is a realm of "real objects" amongst which we live and into which we inquire as a community, but about which we ourselves as individuals presumably have only imperfect information that can be criticized and augmented by the efforts of others.

This points to a fourth important consideration. Only through reference to the real world as a *common object* and shared focus of our diverse and imperfect epistemic strivings are we able to effect communicative contact with one another. Inquiry and communication alike are geared to the conception of an objective world: a communally shared realm of things that exist strictly "on their own" within which and, more importantly, with reference to which inquiry proceeds. We could not proceed on the basis of the notion that inquiry estimates the character of the real if we were not prepared to presume or postulate from the very outset a reality for these estimates to be estimates of. It would clearly be pointless to devise our characterizations of reality if we did not stand committed from the outset to the proposition that there is a reality to be characterized.

The fifth consideration is that the very idea of inquiry, as we conceive it, would have to be abandoned if the conceptions of "actual reality" and "the real truth" were no longer available to serve their crucial contrasting roles. We could no longer assert: "What we have there is good enough as far as it goes, but it is presumably not 'the whole real truth' of the matter." Without the conception of reality, we could not think of our knowledge in the fallibilistic mode we actually use—as having provisional, tentative, improvable features that constitute a crucial part of the conceptual scheme within whose orbit we operate our concept of inquiry. For our commitment to the mind-independent reality of "the real world" stands together with our acknowledgment that, in principle, any or all of our *present* scientific ideas as to how things work in the world, at *any* present, may well prove to be untenable. The information that we may have about a thing, be it real or presumptive information, is always just that—information *we* lay claim to. We recognize that it varies from person to person. Our attempt at communication and inquiry are thus undergirded by the stance that we communally inhabit a shared world of objectively existing things, a world of "real things" amongst which we live and into which we inquire (but about which we do and must assume that we have only imperfect information at any and every particular stage of the cognitive venture). Our conviction in a reality that lies beyond our imperfect understanding of it (in all the various senses of "lying beyond") roots in our sense of the imperfections of our scientific world picture—its tentativity and potential fallibility. In abandoning our commitment to a mind-independent reality, we would lose the indispensably objective impetus of inquiry.

After all, reality (or the traditional metaphysicians' construction of the concept) is the condition of things answering to "the real truth"; it is the realm of what really is as it really is. The pivotal contrast is between "mere appearance" and "reality as such," between "our picture of reality" and "reality itself," between what actually is and what we merely think (believe, suppose) to be. Our allegiance to the conception of reality, and to the appearance/reality contrast that pivots upon it, roots in the fallibilistic recognition that, at the level of the detailed specifics of scientific theory, anything we presently hold to be the case can possibly turn out otherwise—indeed, certainly will do so if past experience gives any auguries for the future.

Finally, we need the conception of reality in order to operate the causal model of empirical inquiry regarding the real world. Our standard picture of man's place in the scheme of things is predicated on the fundamental idea that there is a real world (however imperfectly our inquiry may characterize it) whose causal operations produce *inter alia* causal impacts upon us, providing the basis of our world picture. Reality is viewed as the causal source and basis of the appearances, the originator and determiner of the phenomena of our cognitively relevant experience. "The real world" is seen as causally operative both in serving as the external molder of thought and as constituting the ultimate arbiter of the adequacy of our theorizing. In summary, then, we need that postulate of an objective order of mind-independent reality for at least six important reasons:

- To preserve the distinction between true and false with respect to factual matters and to operate the idea of truth as agreement with reality.
- To preserve the distinction between appearance and reality, between our *picture* of reality and reality itself.
- To serve as a basis for intersubjective communication.
- To furnish the basis for a shared project of communal inquiry.
- To provide for the fallibilistic view of human knowledge.
- To sustain the causal mode of learning and inquiry and to serve as a basis for the objectivity of experience.

What is at stake here is thus ultimately a principle of practice—though, to be sure, it is thought practice that is at issue. Accordingly, the justification for this fundamental presupposition of objectivity is not *evidential* at all; postulates as such are not based on evidence. Rather, it is practical and instrumentalistic—pragmatic, in short. It is procedural or functional efficacy that is the crux. The justification of this postulate lies in its utility: we need it to operate our conceptual scheme. We could not form our existing conceptions of truth, fact, inquiry, and communication without presupposing the independent reality of an external world. In its absence, we simply could not think of experience and inquiry as we actually do. (What we have here is a "transcendental argument" of sorts, namely, one that argues from the character of our conceptual scheme to the unavoidability of accepting its inherent presuppositions.)

Therefore, our commitment to the mind-independent reality of "the real world" stands alongside our fallibilistic acknowledgment that in principle any or all of our *present* scientific ideas about how things work in the world, at *any* present, may well prove to be untenable. Our conviction of a reality that lies beyond our imperfect understanding of it (in all the various senses of "lying beyond") has roots in the imperfections we sense in our scientific world-picture—its tentativity and potential fallibility. In abandoning this commitment to a mind-independent reality, we would lose the impetus of inquiry. Yet realism's epistemic status is not that of an empirical discovery but of a presupposition whose ultimate justification is a transcendental argument from the very possibility of the projects of communication and inquiry as we typically conduct them.

The presuppositional conception of a mind-independent reality accordingly plays a central and indispensable role in our thought about cognitive matters. It is seen as the epistemological *object* of veridical cognition, in the context of the contrast between "the real" and its "merely phenomenal" appearances. Moreover, it is seen as the target of *telos* of the truth-estimation process at issue in inquiry, providing for a common focus in communication and communal inquiry. (The "real world" thus constitutes the *object* of our cognitive endeavors in both senses of this term—the *objective* at which they are directed and the *purpose* for which they are exerted.) Furthermore, reality is also to be seen as the ontological *source* of cognitive endeavors, affording the existential matrix in which we live and move and have our being—and whose impact upon us is the prime mover for our cognitive efforts. All of these facets of the concept of reality are integrated and unified in the classical doctrine of truth as it corresponds to fact (*adaequatio ad rem*), a doctrine that not merely invites but indeed requires a commitment to mind-independent reality as constituting at once the framework and the object of our cognitive endeavors in science. And their ultimate ratification lies in their role as indispensable presuppositions for our unavoidable practices.

Realism and Objectivity as a Requisite of Communication

Independent reality is functionally pivotal in matters of communication. Subscription to an objective reality is indispensably demanded by any step into the domain of the publicly accessible objects essential to communal inquiry and interpersonal communication about a shared world. We could not establish communicative contact about a common objective item of discussion if our discourse were geared to our own idiosyncratic experiences and those conceptions bound up with them. But the objectivity at issue in our communicative discourse is a matter of its very *status* as putatively communicative, rather than somehow depending on its specific *content*. For the substantive content of a claim about the world in no way tells us whether it is factual or fictional. This is something that we have to determine from its *context,* which means, in effect, that in general it is provided for by a preestablished conventionalized intention to talk about "the real world." This intention to take real objects to be at issue, objects as they actually are, our potentially idiosyncratic conceptions of them quite aside, is fundamental because it is overriding—that is, it overrides all of our other intentions when we embark on the communicative venture. Without this conventionalized intention we should not be able to convey information—or misinformation—to one another about a shared "objective" world that underlies and connects those variable experiences of ours.

If it were not reality as it actually is that we are concerned to discuss, but merely "reality as I conceive it to be," then we could not really manage to agree or disagree with one another. Indeed, we could then just not communicate successfully in the informative mode. We are able to say something about the (real) moon or the (real) Sphinx because of our submission to a fundamental communicative convention or "social contract" to the effect that we *intend* ("mean") to talk about the very thing itself as it "really" is—our own personal conception of it notwithstanding. We adopt the standard policy in communicative discourse of letting the communally established language, rather than whatever specific informative notions and conceptions we may actually "have in mind" on particular occasions, be the decisive factor with regard to the things at issue in our discussions. While in speaking about the Sphinx I do so on the basis of my own conceivably strange conception of what is involved here, I will nevertheless be discussing "the *real* Sphinx" by virtue of the basic conventionalized intention governing our use of referring terms within the wider community.

Any effective venture in communication must be predicated on the fundamental intention to deal with the objective order of this "real world." This fundamental intention of objectification, the intention to discuss "the actual Sphinx" or "the moon itself"—regardless of how untenable one's own *ideas* about it may eventually prove to be—is in fact a basic precondition of the very possibility of communication. If our assertoric commitments did not transcend the information we have on hand, we would never be able to "get in touch" with others about a shared objective world. It is crucial to the communicative enterprise to take the egocentrism-avoiding stance that rejects all claims to a privileged status for *our own* conception of things. In the interests of this stance we are prepared to "discount any misconception" (our own included) about things over a very wide range indeed—that we are committed to the stance that factual disagreements as to the character of things are communicatively irrelevant within very broad limits. No claim is made for the *primacy* of our own conceptions, for their *correctness,* or even for their mere *agreement* with those of others. The fundamental intention to discuss "the thing itself" predominates and overrides any mere dealing with the thing as we conceive it to be. Certainly, that reference to "objectively real things" at work in our discourse does not contemplate a peculiar sort of *thing*—a new *ontological* category of "things-in-themselves." It is simply a shorthand formula for a certain communicative presumption or imputation rooted in an a priori commitment to the idea of a commonality of objective focus—a presumption that is allowed to stand unless and until circumstances arise to render this step untenable.

The possible incorrectness of our conceptions is venial in this regard. For if we were to set up our own conception of things as somehow definitive and decisive, we would at once erect a barrier not only to further inquiry but—no less importantly—to the prospect of successful communication with one another. Communication could then only proceed with the wisdom of hindsight—at the end of a long process of tentative checks. "Aha," I can say at the end of a long exchange—and then only—"*now* I can see (or, at least, can plausibly *conjecture*) what it is that was being talked about." Communicative contact would be realized only in the generally problematic situation where extensive exchange indicates retrospectively that a consilience of views exists so that there has been an *identity* of conceptions all along. And we would always stand on very shaky ground. For no matter how far we push our investigation into the issue of an identity of conceptions, the prospect of a divergence lying just around the corner—waiting to be discovered if only we pursued the matter just a bit further—can never be precluded. One could never advance the issue of the identity of focus past the status of a more or less well-grounded *assumption*. And then any so-called communication would no longer be an exchange of information but a tissue of frail conjectures. The communicative enterprise would become a vast inductive project—a complex exercise in theory building, leading tentatively and provisionally toward something that, in fact, the imputational groundwork of our language enables us to presuppose from the very outset.[3]

The fundamental convention of a shared social insistence on communicating—the commitment to an objective world of real things—affords the crucially requisite common focus indispensable to any genuine communication. What links my discourse topically with that of my interlocutors is our common subscription to the a priori presumption (a defeasible presumption, to be sure) that we are both talking about a shared thing, our own possible misconceptions of it notwithstanding. The commitment to *objectivity* is indispensable for any prospect of effective discourse with one another about a shared world of "real things" regarding which none of us is in a position to claim privileged access. This commitment establishes a need to "distance" ourselves from things, that is, to acknowledge the prospect of a discrepancy between our (potentially idiosyncratic) conceptions of things and the true character of these things as they exist objectively in "the real world." And the conceptualizing of a mind-independent reality is the ever-present mechanism by which this crucially important distancing is accomplished.

However, maintaining this stance means that we are never entitled to claim to have exhausted a thing *au fond* in cognitive regards, to have managed to bring it wholly within our epistemic grasp. For to make this claim would, in effect, be to *identify* "the thing at issue" purely in terms of "our own conception of it," and identification would effectively remove the former item (the thing itself) from the stage of consideration as an independent entity in its own right, by endowing our conception with decisively determinative force. And this would lead straightaway to the unacceptable result of a cognitive solipsism that would preclude reference to intersubjectively identifiable particulars, and would thus block the possibility of interpersonal communication and communal inquiry.

What we have here is a "transcendental argument" of sorts from the character of our conceptual scheme to the acceptability of its inherent presuppositions. The argument has the following generic structure: If you want to achieve certain communicative ends, then you must proceed on the basis of certain substantive commitments of a realistic and objectivistic sort. The fact is that our concept of a *real thing* is such that it provides a fixed point, a stable center around which communication revolves, an invariant focus of potentially diverse conceptions. What is to be determinative, decisive, definitive of the things at issue in my discourse is not my conception, or yours, or indeed anyone's conception at all. The conventionalized intention to a discursive coordination of *reference* means that a coordination of *conceptions* is not decisive for the possibility of communication. For your statements about a thing will and should convey something to me even if my conception of it is altogether different from yours. To communicate we need not take ourselves to share views of the world, but only to take the stance that we share the world being discussed—what matters is the things taken to be at issue, not our opinions about them. This commitment to an objective reality underlying the diversified data at hand is indispensably demanded by any step into the domain of the publicly accessible objects essential to communal inquiry and interpersonal communication about a shared world. We could not establish communicative contact about a common objective item of discussion if our discourse were geared to the substance of our own idiosyncratic ideas and conceptions.

Any and all pretensions to the primacy and predominance, let alone the definitive correctness, of our own conceptions regarding the realm of the real must be set aside in the context of communication. In communication about things, we must be able to exchange information about them with our contemporaries and to transmit information about them to our successors. And we must be in a position to do this while recognizing that *their* conceptions of things may not only be radically different from *ours* but conceivably also rightly different. Thus, it is a crucial precondition of the possibility of successful communication about things that we must avoid laying any claim either to the completeness or even to the ultimate correctness of our own conception of any of the things at issue. This renders critically important *that* (and understandably *why*) conceptions are not pivotal for communicative purposes. Our discourse *reflects* our conceptions and perhaps *conveys* them, but it is not substantively *about* them. We thus deliberately abstain from any claim that our own conception is definitive if we are to engage successfully in discourse. We deliberately put the whole matter of conceptions aside—abstracting from the question of the agreement of my conception with yours, and all the more from the issue of which one of us has the right conception. This sort of epistemic humility is the price we pay for keeping the channels of communication open.

But why embark on the objectivity-presupposing projects of inquiry and communication at all? Why not settle back in comfortable abstention from this whole complex business? The answer is straightforward. The impetus to inquiry for knowledge acquisition reflects the most practical of imperatives. Our need for *intellectual* accommodation in this world is no less pressing and no less *practical* than our need for physical accommodation. But in both cases we do not want just some house or other; we want one that is well built, one that will not be blown down by the first wind to sweep along. Skeptics from antiquity onward have always said, "Forget about those abstruse theoretical issues; focus on your practical needs." They overlook the crucial fact that an intellectual accommodation to the world is itself one of our deepest practical needs—that in a position of ignorance or cognitive dissonance we cannot function satisfactorily.

After all, the project of cognitive development is not optional—at any rate not for us humans. Its rationale lies in the most practical and prudent of considerations, since it is only by traveling the path of inquiry that we can arrive at the sorts of good reasons capable of meeting the demands of a "*rational* animal." Man has evolved within nature into the ecological niche of an intelligent being. In consequence, the need for understanding, for "knowing one's way about," is one of the most fundamental demands of the human condition. The practical benefits of knowledge, on the other hand, relate to its role in guiding the processes by which we satisfy our (noncognitive) needs and wants. The satisfaction of our needs for food, shelter, protection against the elements, and security against natural and human hazards all require information. And the satisfaction of mere desiderata comes into it as well. We can, do, and must put knowledge to work to facilitate the attainment of our goals, guiding our actions and activities in this world into productive and rewarding lines. And this is where the practical payoff of the information we secure through inquiry and communication comes into play. Here, again, pragmatic considerations are paramount.

Only by subscribing to that fundamental reality postulate can we take the sort of view of experience, inquiry, and communication that we in fact have. Without it, the entire conceptual framework of our thinking about the world and our place in it would come crashing down. The validation of those communication-enabling presuppositions lies in this very fact. It is a practical validation. The utility of a commitment to objective reality within the context of our cognitive and practical endeavors is such that even if it were not there, we would have to invent it. Did we perhaps do so? Can it be that nothing more than an intellectual artifact is at issue? Does that underlying praxis itself admit of some further and deeper justification? But how can the pragmatic basis of our concept of reality by itself provide an adequate validation for this crucial resource of communication and inquiry? A "validation" in terms of functional utility establishes our claims to mind-independent reality not by the cognitive route of learning but by the pragmatic route of an indispensably useful postulation. Crucial though this may be, it clearly cannot be the *entire* story.

The Role of Presumption

To clarify the pragmatic rationale of realism, consider a cat-on-the-mat experience where "I take myself to be seeing a cat on the mat." On its basis I would arrive quite unproblematically at the following contentions:

It seems plausible to suppose that there is a cat on the mat.
There is presumably a cat on the mat.

To claim unqualified assurance that a cat is indeed on the mat would be stretching matters too far. Classical skepticism is right on this, that there is a possibility of illusion or delusion—that something controversial might be being done with mirrors or puppets or some other such thing. But the indicated pro-inclination toward the theses at issue is certainly warranted. Conclusiveness may be absent, but plausibility is certainly there.

Yet how is one to get beyond such tentativity? To step from that visual experience to an objective factual claim, such as

there actually is a cat there,
there actually is a mat there, and
the cat is actually emplaced on the mat

is a move that can be made—but not without further ado. Let us consider what else is required here.

The position at issue is a "direct realism" of sorts. The step from a sensory experience ("I take myself to be seeing a cat") to an objective factual claim ("There is a cat over there and I am looking at it") is operationally direct but epistemically mediated. And it is mediated not by an *inference* but by a *policy*, namely, the policy of trusting one's own senses. This policy itself is based neither on wishful thinking nor on arbitrary decisions: it emerges in the school of praxis from the consideration that a long course of experience has taught us that our senses generally guide us aright—that the indications of visual experience, unlike, say, those of dream experience, generally provide reliable information that can be implemented in practice.

But how would this emergence of policy validation from a body of experience work in practice? The concept of presumption is the key that unlocks this issue. The classical theories of perception from Descartes to the sense-datum theorists of the first half of the twentieth century all involve a common difficulty. For all of them saw a real and deep problem to be rooted in the following question:

Under what circumstances are our actual experiences genuinely veridical? In particular: which facts about the perceptual situation validate the move from "I (take myself to) see a cat on the mat" to "There is a cat on the mat"? How are we to mon-itor the appropriateness of the step from "perceptual experi-ences" to actual perceptions of real things-in-the-world, seeing that experience is by its very nature something personal and subjective.

The traditional theories of perception all face the roadblock of the problem: How do we get from here to there, from personal and sub-jective experience to warranted claims of objective fact?

However, what all these theories ignore is the fact that in actual practice we operate within the setting of a conceptual scheme that re-verses the burden of proof here: that our perceptions (and concep-tions) are standardly treated as innocent until proven guilty. The whole course of relevant experience is such that the standing pre-sumption is on their side. The indications of experience are taken as true provisionally—allowed to stand until such time (if ever) that concrete evidential counterindications come into view. Barring indi-cations to the contrary, we can and do move immediately and un-problematically from "I take myself to be seeing a cat on the mat" to "There really is a cat on the mat and I actually see it there." But what is at issue here is not an *inference* (or a deriving) from determinable facts but a mere *presumption* (a taking to be). The transition from sub-jectivity to objectivity is automatic; though, to be sure, it is always pro-visional, that is, subject to the proviso that all goes as it ought. For un-less and until something goes amiss—that is, unless there is a mishap of some sort—those "subjective percepts" are standardly allowed to count as "objective facts."

To be sure, there is no prospect of making an inventory of the nec-essary conditions here. Life is too complex: neither in making asser-tions nor in driving an automobile can one provide a comprehensive advance survey of possible accidents and list all the things that could possibly go wrong. But the key point is that the linkage between ap-pearance and reality is neither conceptual nor causal: it is the product of a pragmatic policy in the management of information, a ground rule of presumption that governs our epistemic practice.

With presumption we *take* to be so what we could not otherwise *derive.* This idea of such presumptive "taking" is a crucial aspect of our language-deploying discursive practice. For presumptively justified beliefs are the raw materials of cognition. They represent contentions that—in the absence of preestablished counterindications—are acceptable to us "until further notice," thus permitting us to make a start in the venture of cognitive justification without the benefit of prejustified materials. Such presumptions are defeasible alright, vulnerable to being overturned, but only by something else yet more secure, some other preestablished conflicting consideration. They are entitled to remain in place until displaced by something better. Accordingly, their impetus averts the dire consequences that would ensue if any and every cogent process of rational deliberation required inputs that themselves had to be authenticated by a prior process of rational deliberation—in which case the whole process could never get under way.

The consideration that we *must* proceed in the way of objectivity-presuming cognition as a matter of the functional requisites of our situation because there is just no viable alternative if our aims are to be attained and our needs and purposes served stops short of being altogether conclusive. For it does not offer us any assurance that we will actually succeed in our endeavor if we do proceed in this way; it just has it that we will not succeed if we do not. So the issue of actual effectiveness remains undecided and a nagging doubt still remains, one that roots in the challenge "Let it be granted that this line of approach provides a cogent practical argument. All this shows only that realism is *useful*—perhaps so much so as to be effectively indispensable for us. But does that make it *true*? Is there any rational warrant for it over and above the mere fact of its utility?"

Indispensability aside, what is it that justifies making presumptions, seeing that they are not established truths? The answer lies substantially in procedurally *practical* considerations. Presumptions arise in contexts where we have questions and need answers. It is a matter of *faute de mieux,* of this or nothing (or at any rate nothing better). Presumption is a thought instrumentality that so functions as to make it possible for us to do the best we can in circumstances where something must be done. Presumption affords yet another instance where practical considerations play a leading role on the stage of our cognitive and communicative practice. For presumption is, in the end, a practical device whose rationale of validation lies on the order of pragmatic considerations.

The obvious and evident advantage of presumption as an epistemic recourse is that it enables us vastly to extend the range of questions we are able to answer. It affords an instrument that enables us to extract a maximum of information from communicative situations. Presumption, in sum, is an ultimately pragmatic resource. To be sure, its evident disadvantage is that the answers that we obtain by its means are given not in the clarion tones of knowledge and assertion but in the more hesitant and uncertain tones of presumption and probability. We thus do not get the advantages of presumption without an accompanying negativity. Here, as elsewhere, we cannot have our cake and eat it too.

We proceed in cognitive contexts in much the same manner that banks proceed in financial contexts. We extend credit to others, doing so at first to a relatively modest extent. When and as they comport themselves in a way that indicates that this credit was warranted, we then extend more. By responding to trust in a "responsible" way—proceeding to amortize the credit one already has—one can increase one's credit rating in cognitive contexts, much as in financial ones.

In trusting the senses, in relying on other people, *and even in being rational,* we always run a risk. Whenever in life we place our faith in something, we run a risk of being let down and disappointed. Nevertheless, it seems perfectly reasonable to bet on the general trustworthiness of the senses, the general reliability of our fellow people, and the general utility of reason. In such matters, no absolute guarantees can be had. But one may as well venture, for if venturing fails the cause is lost anyhow—we have no more promising alternative to turn to. There is little choice about the matter: it is a case of "this or nothing." If we want answers to factual questions, we have no real alternative but to trust in the cognitively cooperative disposition of the natural order of things. We cannot preestablish the appropriateness of this trust by somehow demonstrating, in advance of events, that our trust is actually warranted. Rather, its rationale is that without it we remove the basis on which alone creatures such as ourselves can confidently live a life of effective thought and action. In such cases, pragmatic rationality urges us to gamble on trust in reason, not because it cannot fail us, but because in so doing little is to be lost and much to be gained. A general policy of judicious trust is eminently cost effective in yielding useful results in matters of cognition.

The Role of Retrovalidation

Further difficulties yet remain, of course: Pragmatic utility is all very good, but what of validity? What sorts of considerations *validate* our particular presumptions as such: how is it that they become *entitled* to this epistemic status? The crux of the answer has already been foreshadowed. A two-fold process is involved. Initially, it is a matter of the generic need for answers to our questions: of being so circumstanced that if we are willing to presume we are able to get anything. But ultimately we go beyond such this-or-nothing consideration, and the validity of a presumption emerges ex post facto through the utility (both cognitive and practical) of the results it yields. We advance from "this or nothing" to "this or nothing that is determinably better." Legitimation is thus available, albeit only through experiential *retrovalidation,* retrospective validation in the light of eventual experience. It is a matter of learning that a certain issue is more effective in meeting the needs of the situation than its available alternatives. Initially, we look to promise and potential, but what counts in the end is applicative efficacy.

The fact is that our cognitive practices have a fundamentally economic rationale. They are all cost effective within the setting of the project of inquiry to which we stand committed (by our place in the world's scheme of things). Presumptions are the instrument through which we achieve a favorable balance of trade in the complex trade-offs between ignorance of fact and mistake of belief—between unknowing and error.

The starting point of our justificatory reasoning was a basic project-facilitating postulation. Yet this does not tell the whole story. For there is also the no less important fact that this postulation obtains a vindicating retrojustification because the farther we proceed on this basis, the more its obvious appropriateness comes to light. With the wisdom of hindsight we come to see with increasing clarity that the project that these presuppositions render possible is an eminently successful one. The pragmatic turn does crucially important work here in putting at our disposal a style of justificatory argumentation that manages to be cyclical without vitiating circularity. What is at issue is a matter of unavoidable presumptions whose specific mode of implementation is ultimately retrovalidated through experience.

We want and need objective information about "the real world." This information is not to be had directly, of course, without the epistemic mediation of experience. So we treat certain data as evidence— we extend "evidential credit" to them. Through trial and error we learn that some data are indeed credit worthy, so we "increase their credit limit" and rely on them more extensively. And, of course, to use those data as evidence is to build up a picture of the world, a picture that shows, with the "wisdom of hindsight," how appropriate it was for us to have used those evidential data in the first place.

Charles S. Peirce frames the issue with his characteristic clarity: "It may be asked how I know that there are reals. If this hypothesis is the sole support of my method of inquiry, my method of inquiry must not be used to support my hypothesis."[4] He poses exactly the right question. Yet while this reality hypothesis is indeed not a product of inquiry but a presupposition for it, nevertheless, it is one whose justification ultimately stands or falls on the success of the inquiries it facilitates. Its validation cannot be preestablished through evidence but can only be provided ex post facto through the justificatory impetus of successful implementation. On this basis, the substantive picture of nature's ways that is secured through our empirical inquiries is itself ultimately justified, retrospectively, through affording us with the presuppositions on whose basis inquiry proceeds. As we proceed to develop science there must come a retrojustificatory "closing of the circle." The world picture that science delivers must eventually explain how creatures such as ourselves, emplaced in the world as we are and investigating it by the processes we actually use, should do fairly well at developing a workable view of that world. As we saw in the preceding chapter's discussion of "rational selection," the "validation of scientific method" must and can in the end itself become scientifically validated. Though the process is cyclic and circular, there is nothing vicious and vitiating about it.

The rational structure of this pragmatic validation of realism accordingly looks like this:

1. We use various sorts of experiential data as evidence of objective fact.

2. We do this in the first instance for purely *practical* reasons, *faute de mieux,* because only by proceeding in this way can we hope to resolve our questions with any degree of rational satisfaction (functional validation).

3. But as we proceed two things happen:

   a. On the pragmatic side we find that we obtain a world picture on whose basis we can operate effectively (pragmatic revalidation).

   b. On the cognitive side we find that we arrive at a picture of the world that can itself provide an explanation of how it is that we are encouraged to get things (roughly) right—that we are in fact justified in using our phenomenal data as data of objective fact (explanatory revalidation).

The success at issue in this pragmatic perspective is twofold—that which applies to understanding (cognition) and that which regards application (praxis). And it is the latter that ultimately justifies and retrospectively validates our evidential proceedings.

We accordingly arrive at the overall situation of dual "retrojustification." For all the presuppositions of inquiry are ultimately justified because a "wisdom of hindsight" enables us to see that by their means we have been able to achieve both practical success and a theoretical understanding of our place in the world's scheme of things. Here, successful practical implementation is needed as an extra-theoretical quality control of our theorizing. And the capacity of our scientifically devised view of the world to explain how it is that a creature constituted as we are, operating by the means of inquiry that we employ, and operating within an environment such as ours, can ultimately devise a relatively accurate view of the world is also critical for the validation of our knowledge.[5] The closing of these inquiry-geared loops validates, retrospectively, those realistic presuppositions or postulations that made the whole process of inquiry possible in the first place. Realism thus emerges as a presupposition-affording postulate for inquiry—a postulation whose ultimate legitimation eventuates retrospectively through the results, both practical and cognitive, that the process of inquiry based on those yet-to-be-justified presuppositions is able to achieve.

The retroactive component of the justification at issue is critical for our purposes here: That the a priori presumption of realism could be validated by the "essential presupposition" argument that if we do not proceed in this way, then success in the projects at issue (inquiry and communication) simply becomes impossible. So far, so good. But not quite enough. For this reasoning pivots the matter on the issue of the mere possibility of success and does nothing to extend any sort of assurance that success will actually be attained. (We remain at the level of necessary conditions without achieving a sufficiency that can only be realized ex post facto, after we actually proceed with the process of inquiring. That this is achievable to a reasonable degree has to be a matter of actual discovery. And it is here that the factor of pragmatic efficacy at issue with such retrojustification comes to play its critical role.

Retrospect

Let us review the overall line of deliberation. Metaphysical realism—the doctrine that there is a mind-independent reality and that our experience can provide us with a firm cognitive grip on it—does not represent a learned fact but a presuppositional postulate. As such, it has a complex justification that unfolds in two phases.

The first, initial phase is prospective, proceeding with a view to the functional necessity of *taking* this position—its purpose-dictated inevitability. For this step alone renders possible a whole range of activities relating to inquiry and to communication that is of the highest utility for us—and, indeed, is a practical necessity. In possibilizing[6] a host of purpose-mandated activities—that is, bringing them within the range of the feasible—the postulate of metaphysical realism obtains its initial justification in the practical order of reasoning. However, such an initial functional justification of metaphysical realism is good but not good enough. So a second phase of justification goes further—indispensably, albeit only retrospectively. It proceeds by noting that when (which is to say *after*) we actually engage in the goal-directed practice that the postulate in question possibilizes, our applicative and explanatory efforts are, in fact, attended by success—that making the initial postulate has an immense pragmatic payoff, since what is involved is not just pragmatic utility but pragmatic efficacy. This issue of actual efficacy is ultimately crucial for the justification of the practical postulate at issue.

In this way, then, the overall strategy of validation has two phases—the one preliminary and prospective, the other substantiative and retrospective. That we must take on a commitment to realism is presupposed for the conduct of inquiry as we understand it. However, that we fare well through proceeding in this way in matters of communication and inquiry is something that has the status of an ex post facto discovery. Insofar as actual evidentiation is asked for, we have all that we can reasonably hope to obtain, given the inevitable realities of the situation we confront in this domain.

So in seeking for the most plausible rationale for realism, we enter the region of pragmatic presuppositions retrojustified through their applicative and implementational efficacy. The utility of the conception of reality is so great and the service it renders so important that if it were not already there we would have to invent it. But the pragmatic success that ensues systematically when we put this conception to work serves to show that in doing so we have not proceeded capriciously.[7]

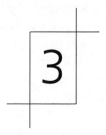

3

Presuppositional Realism and Justificatory Idealism

Realism and Incapacity

Realism is the doctrine that the objects of our knowledge are generally mind-independent because what exists will in general do so in ways unaffected by what mind-endowed beings think about it. Idealism, by contrast, is the doctrine that the way things are is in general dependent on what and how minds think about it. These two doctrines are usually viewed as diametrical opposites locked into a position of conflict that extends through nearly the whole of the history of philosophy.

Often, however—and in metaphysics almost always—when discordant doctrines manage to maintain themselves over many generations, it transpires that there is much to be said on all sides and that the most appropriate and tenable view of the matter is one that combines the best elements of both. Accordingly, the challenge that confronts the metaphysician in such cases is the shaping of a more complex doctrine that manages to effect a higher synthesis among the conflicting contentions by introducing whatever distinctions and sophistications are needed for a reconciliation that accommodates the strong points of each rival position. This chapter endeavors to implement such a compromise with respect to realism and idealism.

What is perhaps the most effective impetus to realism lies in the limitations of man's intellect, pivoting on the circumstances that the features of real things inevitably outrun our cognitive reach. In placing some crucial aspects of the real together outside the effective range of mind, realism speaks for a position that sees mind independence as a salient feature of the real. The very fact of fallibilism and limitedness—of our absolute confidence that our putative knowledge does *not* do full justice to the truth, the whole truth, and nothing but the truth about what reality actually is—is surely one of the best arguments for a realism that pivots on the basic idea that there is more to reality than we humans do or can know. While traditional scientific realists generally see the basis for realism in the substantive knowledge of the sciences, the present metaphysical realism, by contrast, sees its basis in our realization of the inevitable *shortcomings* of our knowledge—scientific knowledge included.

This epistemic approach accordingly preempts one significant sort of skeptical objection. If we are mistaken about the reach of our cognitive powers—if they do not adequately grasp "the way things really are"—then this very circumstance clearly *bolsters* the case for the sort of realism now at issue. The cognitive intractability of things is something about which, in principle, we cannot delude ourselves altogether, since such delusion would illustrate rather than abrogate the fact of a reality independent of ourselves. The very inadequacy of our knowledge is one of the most salient tokens there is of a reality out there that lies beyond the inadequate gropings of mind. It is the very limitation of our knowledge of things—our recognition that reality extends beyond the horizons of what we can possible know or even conjecture about it—that betokens the mind independence of the real.

A meaningful realism can only exist in a state of tension. For the only reality worth having is one that is in some degree knowable. So it is the very limitation of our knowledge—our recognition that there is more to reality than what we do and can know or ever conjecture about it—that speaks for the mind independence of the real. It is important to counter the skeptic by stressing that the human mind is sufficiently well attuned to reality that *some* knowledge of reality is possible. But it is no less important to join with realists in stressing the independent character of reality, acknowledging that reality has a depth and complexity that outruns the reach of mind.

The Complexity of Reals

As we standardly think about particulars within the conceptual framework of our factual deliberation and discourse, *any* real, concrete particular has more features and facets than it will ever actually manifest in experience. After all, concrete things have more properties not only than they ever *will* manifest but also than they ever *can* possibly actually manifest. The existence of this latent (hidden, occult) sector is a crucial feature of our conception of a real thing. Neither in fact nor in thought can we ever simply put it away. To say of this apple that its only features are those it actually manifests is to run afoul of our conception of an apple because there has to be more to it than just exactly that. To deny—or even merely to refuse to be committed to the claim—that it *would* manifest particular features *if* certain conditions came about (for example, that it would have such-and-such a taste if eaten) is to be driven to withdrawing the claim that it is an apple. The latent, implicit ramifications of our objective factual claims regarding something real is potentially endless. The totality of facts about a thing—about any real thing whatsoever—is in principle inexhaustible, and the complexity of real things is in consequence descriptively unfathomable. Endlessly many true descriptive remarks can be made about any particular actual concrete object. For example, take a stone. Consider its physical features: its shape, surface texture, and chemistry. Consider its causal background: its subsequent genesis and history. Consider its multitude of functional aspects as relevant to its uses by the stonemason, the architect, or the landscape decorator. There is, after all, no end to the perspectives of consideration that we can bring to bear on things. The botanist, herbiculturist landscape gardener, farmer, painter, and real estate appraiser will operate from different cognitive "points of view" in describing one selfsame vegetable garden. And there is in principle no theoretical limit to the lines of consideration available to provide descriptive perspective on a thing.

The properties of any real thing are literally open ended: we can always discover more of them. Even if we were (surely mistakenly!) to view the world as inherently finitistic—espousing a Keynesian principle of "limited variety" to the effect that nature can be portrayed descriptively with the materials of a finite taxonomic scheme—there will still be no guarantee that the progress of science will not lead *ad infinitum* to changes of mind regarding this finite register of descriptive materials. And this conforms exactly to our expectation in these matters. For where the real things of the world are concerned, we expect not only to learn more about them in the course of scientific inquiry but *to have to change our minds about their nature and modes of comportment.* Be the items at issue elm trees, or volcanoes, or quarks, we have every expectation that in the course of future scientific progress people will come to think about their origin and their properties differently from the way we ourselves do at this juncture.

How one characterizes real things can accordingly become more *extensive* without thereby becoming more *complete.* New descriptive features continually come into view as knowledge progresses. (Given the state of knowledge at the time, Caesar not only did not know but could not have known that his sword contained tungsten.) Real things are—and by their very nature must be—such that their actual nature outruns any particular description of it that we might venture.

It follows from these considerations that we can never justifiably claim to be in a position to articulate "the whole truth" about a real thing. The domain of thing-characterizing fact inevitably transcends the limits of our capacity to *express* it, and *a fortiori* those of our capacity to canvas completely. In the description of concrete particulars we are caught up in an inexhaustible detail: There are always bound to be more descriptive facts about real things than we are able to capture with our linguistic machinery: the real encompasses more than we can manage to say about it—now or ever.

The Progressive Nature of Knowledge

The existence of this latent (hidden, occult) sector is a crucial element of our conception of a real thing. In this regard, however, real things differ in an interesting and important way from fictive ones. To make this difference plain, it is useful to distinguish between two types of information about a thing—namely, that which is *generic* and that which is not. Generic information tells about those features of a thing that it has in common with everything else of its natural kind or type; for example, a particular snowflake will share with all others certain facts about its structure, its hexagonal form, its chemical composition, and its melting point. It will also have various properties that it does not share with other members in its classificatory order—its particular shape, for example, or the angular momentum of its descent. These are its nongeneric features.

Now, a key about *fictional* particulars is that they are of finite cognitive depth. In discoursing about them we shall ultimately run out of steam when talking about their generic features. A point will always be reached when one cannot say anything further that is characteristically new about them—presenting nongeneric information that is not inferentially implicit in what has already been said. New *generic* information can, of course, always be forthcoming through the progress of science. When we learn more about coal-in-general, then we know more about the coal in Sherlock Holmes's grate. But the finiteness of its cognitive depth means that the presentation of ampliatively novel *nongeneric* information must by the very nature of the case come to a stop when fictional things are at issue.

With *real* things, on the other hand, there is no reason of principle why the provision of nongenerically idiosyncratic information need ever be terminated. On the contrary, we have every reason to presume these things to be cognitively inexhaustible. The prospect of discovery is open ended here. A precommitment to its possession of description-transcending features—no matter how far description is pushed—is essential to our conception of a real thing. Something whose character was exhaustible by descriptive characterization would thereby be marked as fictional rather than real.[1]

This cognitive opacity of real things means that we are not—and never will be—in a position to evade or abolish the contrast between "things as we think them to be" and "things as they actually and truly are." Its susceptibility to further elaborate detail—and to changes of mind regarding this further detail—is built into our very conception of a "real thing." To be a real thing is to be something about which we can always, in principle, acquire further new information—information that may not only supplement but even correct what has previously been acquired. Further inquiry can always, in theory, lead us to recognize the error of our earlier ways of thinking about things—even when thoroughly familiar things are at issue. It is, after all, a fact of life that scientific progress generally entails fundamental changes of mind about how things work in the world. And, of course, what is true of us will be true of all other finite knowers as well.

Hidden Depths: Realism and Objectivity

The fact that we do and should always think of real things as having hidden depths inaccessible to us finite knowers, that they are always to some extent cognitively opaque to us, has important ramifications that reach to the very heart of the theory of communication. Any particular thing—the moon, for example—is such that two related but critically different versions can be contemplated: The moon, the actual moon as it "really" is; and the moon as somebody (you or I or the Babylonians) conceives of it.

The crucial fact to note in this regard is that it is virtually always the thing itself that we *intend* to communicate or think (that is, self-communicate) about, the thing *as it is,* and not the thing *as somebody conceives of it.* Yet we cannot but recognize the justice of Kant's teaching that the "I think" (I maintain, assert) is an ever-present implicit accompaniment of every claim or contention that we make. This factor of attributability dogs our every assertion and opens up the unavoidable prospect of "getting it wrong."

Communication requires not only common *concepts* but common *topics,* shared items of discussion. However, this fundamental objectivity-intent—the determination to discuss "the moon itself" (the real moon) regardless of how untenable one's own *ideas* about it may eventually prove to be—is a basic precondition of the very possibility of communication. It is crucial to the communicative enterprise to take the egocentrism-avoiding stance of an epistemological Copernicanism that rejects all claims to a privileged status for *our own* conception of things. Such a conviction roots in the fact that we are prepared to "discount any misconceptions" (our own included) about things over a very wide range indeed—that we are committed to the stance that factual disagreements as to the character of things are communicatively irrelevant within enormously broad limits.

We are able to say something about the (real) Sphinx thanks to our subscribing to a fundamental communicative convention: we *intend* to talk about the very thing itself as it "really" is, our own private conception of it notwithstanding. When I speak about the Sphinx, even though I do so on the basis of my own conception of it, I will nevertheless be taken to be discussing "the *real* Sphinx" because of the conventionalized intention contained in the referring terms.

Any pretensions to the predominance—let alone the correctness—of our own potentially idiosyncratic conceptions about things must be put aside in the context of communication. The fundamental intention to deal with the objective order of this "real world" is crucial. If our assertoric commitments did not transcend the information we ourselves have on hand, we would never be able to "get in touch" with others about a shared objective world. We do not—cannot—stake any claim to the *primacy* of our conceptions, or to the *correctness* of our conceptions, or even to the mere *agreement* of our conceptions with those of others. The fundamental intention to discuss "the thing itself" predominates and overrides any mere dealing with the thing as we ourselves conceive of it.

The information that we may have about a thing—be it real or presumptive information—is always just that, namely, information that *we* lay claim to. We cannot but recognize that it is person relative and in general person differentiated. Our attempts at communication and inquiry are thus undergirded by an information-transcending stance—the stance that we communally inhabit a shared world of objectively existing things—a world of "real things" amongst which we live and into which we inquire but about which we do and must presume ourselves to have only imperfect information at every stage of the cognitive venture. This is not something we learn; experience can never reveal it to us. We simply postulate or presuppose that we will be able to put experience to cognitive use. Its epistemic status is not that of an empirical discovery but of a *presupposition* that is a product of a transcendental argument for the very possibility of communication or inquiry as we standardly conceive of it.

What is at issue here is not discovery but an *imputation*. The element of community, of identity of focus, is not a matter of learning from experience, but of an a priori predetermination inherent in our approach to language use. We do not *infer* things as being real and objective from our phenomenal data but establish our perception as authentic perception *of* genuine objects through the fact that these objects are given—or rather, *taken*—as real and objectively existing things in the first place.[2] Objectivity is not deduced but imputed. We do, no doubt, *purport* our conceptions to be objectively correct, but whether this is indeed so is something we cannot tell with assurance until "all the returns are in"—and this will never occur. This fact renders it critically important *that* (and, understandably, *why*) conceptions are communicatively irrelevant. Our discourse *reflects* our conceptions and perhaps *conveys* them, but it is not in general substantively *about* them but rather about the things in which they actually or supposedly bear.

We thus reach an important conjuncture of ideas. The ontological independence of things—their objectivity and the autonomy of the machinations of mind—is a crucial aspect of realism. And the fact that it lies at the very core of our conception of a real thing that such items project beyond the cognitive reach of mind betokens a conceptual scheme fundamentally committed to objectivity. The only plausible sort of ontology is one that contemplates a realm of reality that outruns the range of knowledge (and, indeed, even of language), adopting the stance that character goes beyond the limits of characterization. It is a salient aspect of the mind-independent status of the objectively real that the features of something real always transcend what we know about it. Indeed, yet further or different facts concerning a real thing can always come to light, and all that we *do* say about it does not exhaust all that *can* and *should* be said about it. Objectivity and its concomitant commitment to a reality beyond our subjective knowledge of it is thus a fundamental feature of our view of our own position in the world's scheme of things.

The Idealistic Dimension of the Rationale of Realism

The conception of a mind-independent reality accordingly plays a central and indispensable role in our thinking about communication and cognition. In both areas alike we seek to offer answers to our questions about how matters stand in this "objective realm," and the contrast between "the real" and its "merely phenomenal" appearances is crucial here. Moreover, this is also seen as the target and *telos* of the truth-estimation process at issue in inquiry, providing for a common focus in communication and communal inquiry. The "real world" thus constitutes the "object" of our cognitive endeavors in both senses of this term—the *objective* at which they are directed and the *purpose* for which they are exerted. And reality is seen as pivotal here, affording the existential matrix in which we move and have our being, and whose impact on us is the prime mover for our cognitive efforts. All of these facets of the concept of reality are integrated and unified in the classical doctrine of truth as it corresponds to fact (*adaequatio ad rem*), a doctrine that only makes sense in the setting of a commitment to mind-independent reality.

Accordingly, the justification for this fundamental presupposition of objectivity is not *evidential* at all; postulates are not based on evidence. Rather, its justification is *functional*. We need this postulate to operate our conceptual scheme. The justification of this postulate accordingly lies in its utility. We could not form our existing conceptions of truth, fact, inquiry, and communication without presupposing the independent reality of an external world. We simply could not think of experience and inquiry as we do.

What we have here is a "transcendental deduction" of the following generic structure: If you want to achieve certain communicative ends, then you must function on the basis of certain substantive commitments of a realistic and objectivistic sort. Our concept of a *real thing* is such that it provides a fixed point, a stable center around which communication revolves, an invariant focus of potentially diverse conceptions. What is to be determinative, decisive, definitive of the things at issue in my discourse is not my conception, or yours, or, indeed, anyone's conception at all. The conventionalized intention to a discursive coordination of *reference* means that a coordination of *conceptions* is not decisive for the possibility of interpersonal communication. Your statements about a thing will and should convey something to me even if my conception of the thing is altogether different from yours. To communicate with one another we need not take ourselves to share views of the world; we need only take the stance that we share the world being discussed. This commitment to an objective reality that underlies the data at hand is indispensably demanded by any step into the domain of the publicly accessible objects essential to communal inquiry and interpersonal communication about a shared world. We could not establish communicative contact about a common, objective item of discussion if our discourse were geared to the substance of our own idiosyncratic ideas and conceptions.

The ontological thesis that there is a mind-independent physical reality to which our inquiries address themselves more or less adequately—and always imperfectly—is the key contention of realism. But on the telling of the presenting analysis, this basic thesis has the epistemic status of a presuppositional postulate that is initially validated by its pragmatic utility and ultimately retrovalidated by the satisfactory results of its implementation (in both practical and theoretical respects). Our commitment to realism is, on this account, initially not a product of our *inquiries* about the world but rather reflects a facet of how we *conceive* the world. The sort of realism contemplated here is accordingly one that pivots on the fact that we *think* of reals in a certain sort of way, and that in fact the very conception of the real is something we employ because doing so merits our ends and purposes. The rationale of a commitment to ontological objectivity is in the final analysis functionally or pragmatically driven. Without a presuppositional commitment to objectivity with its acceptance of a real world independent of ourselves that we share in common, interpersonal communication would become impracticable. Realism, then, is a position to which we are constrained not by the push of evidence but by the pull of purpose. Initially, at any rate, a commitment to realism is an *input* into our investigation of nature rather than an *output* thereof. At bottom, it represents not a discovered fact but a methodological presupposition of our praxis of inquiry; its status is not that of a constitutive (fact-descriptive) *given* but of a regulative (praxis-facilitating) *taken*. Realism is not a factual discovery but a practical postulate justified by its utility or serviceability in the context of our aims and purposes, seeing that if we did not *take* our experience to serve as an indication of facts about an objective order we would not be able to validate any objective claims whatsoever. (To be sure, what we can, and do, ultimately discover is that by taking this realistic stance we are able to develop a praxis of inquiry and communication that proves effective in the conduct of our affairs.)

Now insofar as realism ultimately rests on such pragmatic footing, it is not based on considerations of independent substantiating evidence about how things actually stand in the world but rather on considering, as a matter of practical reasoning, how we do (and must) think about the world within the context of the projects to which we stand committed. In this way, the commitment to a mind-independent reality plays an essentially utilitarian role as providing a functional requisite for our intellectual resources (specifically, for our conceptual scheme in relation to communication and inquiry). Realism thus harks back to the salient contention of classical idealism that values and purposes play a pivotal role in our understanding of the nature of things. And we return also to the characteristic theme of idealism—the active role of the knower not only in the constituting but also in the constitution of what is known. A position of this sort is in business as a realism all right. But seeing that it pivots on the character of our concepts and their modus operandi, the business premises it occupies are actually mortgaged to idealism. The fact that objectivity is the fruit of communicative purpose allows idealism to infiltrate into the realist's domain.

The idealism at issue cuts deeper yet. No doubt, we are firmly and irrevocably committed to the idea that there is a physical realm out there that all scientific inquirers alike inhabit and examine. We hold to a single, uniform physical reality, insisting that all investigations exist within and investigate *it:* this one single shared realism, this one single manifold of physical objects and laws. But this very idea of a single, uniform domain of physical object and laws represents just exactly that—*an idea of ours*. This idea is itself a matter of how we find it convenient and efficient to think about things: it is no more, and no less, than the projection of a theory devised to meet the needs and conveniences of our intellectual situation.

This approach endorses an object-level realism that rests on a presuppositional idealism at the justificatory infralevel. We arrive, paradoxical as it may seem, at a realism that is founded, initially at least, on a fundamentally idealistic basis—a realism whose ultimate *justificatory basis* is ideal.

Conceptual Idealism and the Pivotal Role of Identification for Identity

The pivotal thesis of conceptual idealism is that real things *as we conceive of them* are infused with mind-supplied aspects. It is sometimes said that idealism is predicated on confusing objects with our knowledge of them and conflates the real with our thinking about it. But this charge misses the point. The thesis of a specifically conceptual idealism is not the trivial one that mind makes the *idea* of nature; it is not open to Santayana's complaint against Schopenhauer that "he proclaimed that the world was his idea but meant only (what is undeniable) that his *idea* of the world was his idea." Rather, what is at issue is that mind-patterned conceptions are built into our idea of nature: that the way we standardly conceive of real things is in some crucial respects patterned on our self-conception as mind-endowed agents: we ascribe to the real characteristics in whose conceptual constitution the operations of mind are implicated. In particular, even the concept of a particular individual thing is of this nature. The line of thought at issue can be set out as follows:

- Any real object, anything that actually exists is in principle cognizable. For the item at issue, whatever it is, could not be all it is if it were not identifiable as such.
- Something is cognizable (and identifiable) only under a description. To be real is to be a certain sort of thing—its identity can only be established under a certain sortal characterization.
- Sortalization (characterization, description) and with it identification is a mind-involving operation. It can only be accomplished by mind-endowed beings.

The argument is thus straightforward: The fact that real things must be identifiable means that reality is a matter of existence-as; to exist at all is to exist as a certain sortal type of thing. And sortalization depends on mental operations (as William James rightly maintained, our interests determine our descriptive and classificatory schemata). Accordingly, a realism of identifiable individuals is operatable only on the basis of an idealism of mental capacities in identification, description, and classification.

The very idea of an individual thing—an individualized unit—is thus mind-infected. For to identify something is to characterize it descriptively or to indicate it ostensively or somehow else distinguish it from other things. Identification is thus a process in which one person so acts as to indicate something to a comprehending interlocutor, and all such processes have the common feature that *the attention of a mind is so directed as to be brought to focus upon something.* Accordingly, it should be an unproblematic and indeed even the superficial point that all modes of identification are mind-involving interactions. A basically interpersonal *transaction* is at issue here—namely, describing, discriminating, pointing out, distinguishing, and so forth, all of which invariably have a person as indirect object: they are transactions involving what one agent does for another (or for himself, in the special case).[3] Identity is the correlate of identification, and identification is, by nature, a mentalistic act: "to identify" as an intellectual process and "to be identified" is accordingly a mind-invoking condition. The concept of identification itself contains an intrinsic reference to the directable attention of a comprehending intelligence. Our concepts correlate with norms of application ("use conditions"), and the moral-correlative process called *identification* is inextricably implicated in the concept of an individual thing.

Conceptual idealism is thus predicated on the important distinction between conceptual mind involvingness and explicit mind invokingness, illustrated in the contrast between a *book* and a *dream.* To characterize an object of consideration as a *dream* or a *worry* is explicitly mind-invoking. For dreams and worries exist only where there is dreaming and worrying, which, by their very nature, typify the sorts of things at issue in the thought processes of mind-endowed creatures:

where there are dreams and worries, these must be mind-equipped beings dreaming and worrying. A book, by contrast, seems to be entirely nonmental: books, after all, unlike dreams or worries, are physical objects. If mind-endowed beings were to vanish from the world, dreams and worries would vanish with them—but not books! Even if there were no mind-endowed beings, there could certainly be naturally evolved booklike objects, objects *physically indistinguishable from books as we know them.* Nevertheless, there could not be *books* in a world where minds had never existed. For a book is, by definition, an artifact of a certain purposive (that is, communicative) sort equipped with pages on which "reading material" is printed. Such purposive artifacts all invoke goal-directed processes of a type that can exist only where there are minds. To be a book is to contain *reading material* (words, pictures), and not just *marks.* Such reading material is inherently the sort of thing produced and employed by mind-endowed beings. In sum, to explain adequately what a *book* is we must thus make reference to reading and thereby ultimately to minds.

The point is not that the book is mentalesque as a physical object but rather that to explicate what is involved in characterizing that object as "a book" we must eventually refer to minds and their capabilities, seeing that a book is by its very nature something people read. A world in which there neither are nor ever have been minds can contain objects physically indistinguishable from our books and nails, but books and nails they could not be, since only artifacts created for a certain sort of intelligence-invoking purpose can correctly be so characterized. So, while books, unlike dreams, are not mental items, their conceptualization/characterization must nevertheless in the final analysis be cast in mind-involving terms of reference. And this sort of thing is true of real things in general, since to be real is to be knowable in principle by intelligent, mind-endowed beings. Accordingly, *conceptual* idealism sees mind not as *causal source* of the materials of nature but as indispensably furnishing some of the *interpretative mechanisms,* such as individuality and agency, in whose terms we standardly conceive of them.

Thought or discourse cannot coherently deal with a particular as "a thing as it is in itself" but must consider things under such-and-such a description that we ourselves provide. Objects must be *thought of*—exactly as they must be *seen*—from a perspective or "point of view." (Of course, with thought, unlike seeing, it is an *intellectual* perspective and not an optical one that is at issue: the perspective of a certain family of concepts.) But even as it is trite to say that the *description* of any real thing or state of affairs is conceptually perspectival, it is not hard to see that this must also hold for *identification*. Just as physical objects cannot be seen free from the limitations of a *physical* point of view, so objects of consideration cannot be contemplated or discussed free from the limitations of a conceptual point of view. Just as things must be seen, so they must be conceived of or considered perspectivally: "under a certain description," as current jargon has it, that is, through the mediation of some family of concepts ; if something is to be considered or discussed at all, this must, of course, be done from *some* conceptual perspective or other.

To return to the pivotal point, it is clear that particularity, which depends on identificatory individuation, is thereby something mind involving. Moreover, to be a particular item is to be identifiable as an individual item with a nature and an identity: to be distinguishable as one discrete item in contrast to others. But even as what makes something a book is that it is readable, so what makes something an object in the real world is that it is experienceable. In its very nature, particularity consists in identifiability, distinguishability, discriminability. The prospect of identification is crucial for objectivity: to be an object, even merely an object of consideration, requires having an identity, being individualizable. But all of these processes (identifying, distinguishing, discriminating) are fundamentally mind involving; each involves attention being directed and is accordingly the sort of thing that mind-endowed beings—and only mind-endowed beings—can do. Identification has to be achieved via a selection specification of features only minds can accomplish.

The impact of this argument that identification is mind involving is tempered by the following line of objection:

Let it be granted (says the objector) that your argument has shown that to say "X is *identified*" is to make a mind-referential claim. But this does not mean that "X is *identifiable*" is mind involving. Your approach slurs the crucial distinction between actuality and possibility. For consider the pairs: described/describable, mentioned/mentionable, indicated/indicatable, and identified/identifiable. If one grants that the first member of such a pair is mind-involving, one does not thereby concede that the second member is. Thus, saying that a certain particular is *identified* may well carry a covert reference to a mind, but this does not show that its *identifiability* is mind dependent. Consequently, since generic particularity demands only identifiability and not actual identification, your argument that actual identification is mind involving does not show that *identifiably* is, and so does not suffice to establish the conclusion that particularity is.

It must be granted, of course, that there is no contradiction in saying that there are particulars that are not identified (though obviously an example of one cannot be given). But the impetus of the objection can nevertheless be deflected by recognizing the fundamental difference between identification, on the one hand, and description, indication, and the rest, on the other. For identification is, in the present context, entirely unique and *sui generis* in a way that impedes straightforwardly applying the analogy of actual and potential on which the objection rests. To be sure, it makes perfectly good sense to say of something that it is describable but not described or is indicatable but not indicated. The actual/potential distinction is indeed operative in these cases. *But this is not so with identification:* We cannot in principle meaningfully say of something that it is identifiable but not identified, because saying this would be nonsense. One would be saying explicitly that one does not know what one is speaking of; where the item at issue is not identified there is nothing that we can specifically say about it. Until it has been identified (however imperfectly), we simply are not dealing with a particular individual thing: we cannot appropriately be held to say anything about "it"—not even that it is identifiable. To say this is not, of course, to deny that we can speak of otherwise unspecified particulars, as in a statement like "One of the trees in this forest has treasure buried beneath it." But cases of this sort pose no difficulty for our position. For if indeed there is treasure buried under just one tree, then we have, in effect, succeeded in making an identifying reference to it (as "the tree that has treasure beneath it"); but if there are several trees above the treasure (or none) at all, then there just is no "it" about which we can be said to be speaking: our purportedly identifying reference fails to refer, so that our statement becomes, under these circumstances, semantically untenable.

Conclusion

Only two conceptual routes lead into the realm of the particular, that of actual identification and that of potential identifiability. Identification is conceptually mind invoking because it is an attention-directing, and thus overtly mental, process. Identifiability is implicitly mind involving because of the mentalesque nature of *identification* itself.

It is, however, important in this connection to reemphasize once more the key distinction between the *ontological* mind dependency of mind invokingness and the *conceptual* mind dependency of mind involvingness. Granted, only identification is mind dependent in the strong sense of mind involvingness, and not identifiably. But that, of course, does not prevent identification from being *conceptually* mind involving—as it indeed is, seeing that the issue pivots on the focusing of attention. To say of something that it is related to minds in a certain way (specifically in the way of admitting being identified by them) is obviously to characterize it in conceptually mind-referring terms (even as describing it as *visible* would be to characterize it in conceptually sight-referring terms).

So even while one must acknowledge that realism is in itself a doctrine that claims for all reals a reality independent of mind and its operations, nevertheless the rationale of such a doctrine—the facts that make its adoption not only possible but appealing—involve a manifold of pivotal considerations in which the operations of mind in relation to the purposive structure of the cognitive enterprise are ineliminably implicated.[4]

Rational Economy and the Evolutionary Impetus

Practical Reason and Its Evaluative and Economic Dimension

In matters of theoretical and practical reason, philosophy traditionally takes a decidedly intellectualist approach. Rationality, as philosophers have generally construed it, is a matter of consistency, coherence, and conformity to the general principles of approved theoretical standards. But while this traditional approach is all very good as far as it goes, it does not do justice to the procedural and action-oriented aspect of the matter. For reason is, at its core, a matter of process, procedure, and action, the intelligent pursuit of appropriate objectives. And this activistic dimension of rationality—inherent in the fact that humans are agents as well as thinkers—has implications that philosophers all too often neglect in their emphasis on such merely theoretical issues as consistency, coherence, and conformity to general principles.

Let us thus focus on practical reason—the use of reason to guide action. Rationality here consists in the efficient and effective pursuit of appropriate goals, and practical reason thus requires and depends on rational evaluation. For it hinges on the evaluative employment of rational reflection and analysis to determine, on the one hand, the inherent appropriateness of goals (inherently evaluative reason) and, on the other, the efficiency and effectiveness of means (instrumentally evaluative reason). Rational adequacy in practical matters requires *efficacy* (can the job be done?) and *efficiency* (can it be done simply and economically?)

The *principle of least effort* is crucial for practical rationality. To expend greater resources on the pursuit of objectives than is required for their prospective realization is a striking form of practical irrationality. And this is where economics comes in, seeing that comparative efficiency and effectiveness are prominent among the ruling standards of economic rationality; the efficient and effective use of resources in the pursuit of one's ends becomes critical, since evaluating the worth of goals ("Is the game worth the candle") is a key aspect of economic rationality. Moreover, those ends themselves must be duly evaluated. A good may be totally legitimate, but it is always only one among others. The meta-evaluative question of how large a place in the sun it merits cannot be avoided. Health is important, but we cannot spend every waking moment pursuing it. Accordingly, both components of means-ends evaluation are indispensable for the assessment of practical rationality. Neither the sagacious pursuit of inappropriate goals nor the ineffectual pursuit of appropriate goals deserves the authorizing stamp of rational approval.

It deserves emphasis in this regard that we do not decide what is valuable for us humans. The human condition, our place in the world's scheme of things, mandates this for us. The fundamental issue here is needs. Our requirement for the air we breathe and for food, shelter, and clothing is a matter of need. To be sure, we can meet these needs in very different ways—but meet them we must. Our wants root in and emerge from our needs. And it is our needs that are the ultimate basis of what can count as appropriate valuation for us.

Practical Rationality Encompasses Theoretical Rationality

A good case can be made for saying that even the prime concerns of theoretical reason—namely, consistency and coherence—are themselves also matters of practical rationality. For information that is inconsistent or incoherent cannot achieve the aims of the enterprise of inquiry that are at issue with theoretical reason. Inconsistent answers ("yes *and* no") to our questions are effectively no answers at all, and incoherent information is information in name only. What is wrong with theoretical incoherence is thus ultimately something pragmatic; it frustrates the cardinal aim of the practical enterprise of inquiry: to provide sensible answers to the questions we need to have answered for the guidance of action.

The primacy of practical reason must accordingly be acknowledged. Theoretical reason itself stands under its sway. After all, inquiry itself is a practice, and in the pursuit of its aims efficacy and effectiveness in goal realization do and must constitute our criteria of procedural adequacy. Already Thomas Aquinas viewed practical reason (*intellectus practicus*) as an extension of theoretical reason (*intellectus speculativus*): *intellectus speculativus per extensionen fit practicus*.[1] As he saw it, practical reason is broader than theoretical reason and embraces it: cognitive practice is a special brand of practice in general, practice whose aim is the accession of information and the resolution of questions. And this essentially pragmatic/fundamentalistic view of the matter is surely correct.

A practicalistic perspective on cognition is thus not only possible but also eminently desirable. Our ideas and beliefs are, after all, the correlates of various methods that we use in the conduct of our cognitive affairs. They are tools we use to solve our problems: answering questions, guiding actions (both theoretical and practical). They can be viewed in their procedural, methodological, use-oriented roles.

We are embarked here on a broadly economic approach—but one that proceeds in terms of a value theory that envisions a generalized "economy of values," and from whose standpoint the traditional economic values (the standard economic costs and benefits) are merely a rather special case. Such an *axiological* value-geared approach sees theoretical rationality as an integral component of that wider rationality that calls for the effective deployment of our limited resources.

The Primacy of Practice

Theoretical reason in the factual area moves toward a conclusion of the form "Such-and-such is in fact the case regarding the world." Practical reason moves toward a conclusion of the form "Such-and-such is to be done." With respect to the employment of a method it is clear that practical reason is the appropriate mode of justification, since the correctness of a method does not reside in its truth (methods and instrumentalities are by their very nature neither true nor false) but in its appropriateness (its suitability to the task at hand). And since the rational espousal of a factual truth must be governed by an appropriate criterion of acceptance, and any such a criterion is in effect methodological and procedural in nature, it follows that in the factual domain practical reason is basic to the theoretical.

But how can the practical justification of a criteriological standard of factual truth proceed? Plainly by showing that "it works." But, of course, "it works" cannot here mean "succeeds in the theoretical/cognitive task of providing truths," which would commit a blatant circularity. Accordingly, "it works" is best and most appropriately to be construed as "works with the practical purpose of action guidance." The manifold of our affective purposes and material satisfaction is no less crucial for truths than the manifold of our theoretical/cognitive purposes.

These considerations indicate that the ultimate metacriterial standard for weighing a criterion of truth acceptance (in the factual area) is not *cognitive* at all, but rather *affective*, and the justificatory reasoning for the test procedure of truth determination represents in the final analysis an appeal not to knowledge, but to feeling. The affective dimension of pain and frustration, of hope and disappointment of expectation—and their opposites—becomes the court of appeal that stands in ultimate judgment of our procedures for deciding questions of factual truth and falsity. In the final analysis, cognition is ancillary to practice, and *feeling* comes to serve as the ultimate arbiter of empirical *knowledge*.

It is worthwhile to review the whole line of reasoning at issue here.

The components of a pragmatic validation of a truth criterion that takes the route of an appeal to experience are as follows:

1. A practical principle of regulative import is invoked to afford the plausibility (not truth) of matters of record.
2. We note (as matters of record) that employment of the truth-criterion C has provided the C-validated propositions p_1, p_2, ...
3. We note (as matters of record) that in various cases we acted on these C-validated propositions.
4. We note (as matters of record) that affectively advantageous results obtained in these cases—at least by and large.
5. We note (as matters of record) that comparably advantageous results did not obtain in those cases where we acted on criterion C', C'', . . . , that are alternative to C.
6. A practical principle of regulative import is invoked to afford the plausibility (not truth) of the claim that the advantageous results that ensued after using C were obtained *because* we employed C. Accordingly, we attribute these results to C and so obtain the essential promise that "C works" in the pragmatic manner suitable for its methodological validation on grounds of "success."
7. We then take the crucially pragmatic step of moving inferentially from the premise that "C works" in this practical/affective sense to the conclusion of the (methodological) appropriateness of C, with the full range of wider implications this carries with it.

Only with this last step—after invoking two practical principles and a great many presumptively factual claims—do we reach our final goal of experientially validating the correctness of the truth-criterion C at issue on the basis of pragmatic consideration.

It is crucially important to notice that this course of pragmatic validation is not in any direct way a pragmatic justification of the acceptance as true of a particular factual thesis or proposition. Rather, it is a justification of a methodology, and its bearing on propositions is altogether indirect. A two-phased process is envisaged: the acceptance of a thesis as true is validated not in pragmatic terms at all, but in terms of the verdict of our normative standards and methods for truth assessment; however, the appropriateness of these standards themselves is, in turn, validated on pragmatic grounds.

The line of thought at work here is straightforward. It pivots on the question, How is one to argue that a criterion of factual truth "works" (from this pragmatic/affective angle)? Now, in theory one can do this either on theoretical grounds or on general principle. In the present case, however, general principles will not avail us. We have no choice but to proceed on the basis of past experience. And such a recourse to the lessons of experience calls for two inputs: (1) information of the matter of record type, and (2) information regarding the attribution of results to procedures. Here, the matters of record at issue must be seen not as *actual* (factual) truths, but as merely *presumptive* data. And the status of an attribution thesis must also be viewed as merely *presumptive* in that it represents a presumption based on postulation. For undergirding this whole warranting process is an appeal to certain practical precepts of procedural justification that define and constitute the very essence of rationality of action.

The experientially pragmatic validation of a criterion of factual truth doubtless encounters difficulties in the way of its implementation. But it would be very ill-advised to see this as grounds for slamming the door on this justificatory approach. For in view of the yet more problems facing its alternatives, this experientially pragmatic route may well qualify, notwithstanding its inherent difficulties, as the most attractive strategy of criterial validation available to us in this mater of a criterion of factual truth.[2] And, in particular, it best enables us to come to terms with the realities of the experiential situation.

However, the experientially pragmatic/experimental justification of a criterion of factual truth along these lines does not constitute anything like a decisive demonstration. For the line of justificatory reasoning in view is based on defeasible presumptions as premises, and it uses reasoning that is itself not demonstrative but merely plausible— in that it can be concerted to demonstration only by the addition of presumption-based postulations. (The maintenance of a distinction between demonstration and plausible reasoning is crucial to the line of justificatory argumentation here.) As concerns the idea that those criterial methods that have served us well in special cases must *in general* succeed better than alternatives, we have no *proof* but merely *suggestive evidence.* All the same, the practical reasoning in view is by no means devoid of the weight of rational warrant. What rationality demands of us is that we do the best we can in the circumstances. And it is unquestionably rational, in epistemic matters as elsewhere, to change from what experience has marked as unsuccessful methods to experientially more favorable-seeming alternatives. To persist with a policy or course of action in the face of continual manifest failure is, after all, the very quintessence of irrationality.

The Given and Its Problems

Classical empiricism maintained that all of our knowledge of the world and its ways roots in the deliverances of sense experience. Against this background Thomas Reid and his congeners in the Scottish School of Common Sense held that in at least some key regards sense experience provides information about the world that is "evident," that is, transparently certain and correct. This view, carried forward into the twentieth century by such philosophers as C. I. Lewis and R. M. Chisholm, has come into strong criticism over the last generation by philosophers (in particular, Wilfred Sellars and his followers) who attacked it as espousing "the myth of the given." As they saw it the transit from subjectivity-geared experience to objective fact is not practicable, and to require its accomplishment would be to throw the doors open to a knowledge-annihilating skepticism.

Now, as we have seen the objective facts purported in our empirical beliefs are never *given* in experience, simply because they inactively transcend anything that mere experience could possibly afford. They are, instead, *taken* on the basis of experiential cues and clues. And just exactly this difference between the given and the taken is what is crucial for the role of experience in yielding our factual knowledge. For it is on the basis of experience-determined cues and clues that we undertake those takings of ours in these matters. But if *taking* is at issue here with its characteristic ventures in postulation and presumption, then what is it that assures that this is not something inappropriate and unjustified? What sort of belief-external quality control have we to ensure the rational appropriateness of our factual beliefs? What thought-external facts can come into operation to monitor the adequacy of our thought about the world and its ways?

At this point the crucial consideration lies in the nature of man as not only a thinker but also a doer, not merely a believer but also an agent. And two factors are pivotal here: (1) our actions are grounded and indeed determined by our beliefs; but (2) once those actions are decided, their outcome is something entirely independent of our wants, wishes, and desires as well as of our opinions, beliefs, and expectations.

Much recent epistemology finds itself stymied by the Davidsonian view that our knowledge of things cannot get outside our beliefs—that the Kantian "I think" is inseparably ubiquitous in relation to our knowledge. But this view has its limits, for there is not only the "I think" of thought but also the whole issue of activity and passivity, of "I act" and "I suffer." And while there is no question that thought grounds our actions, the outcome of these actions is in general thought independent, something outside the conceptual sphere as simply a given feature of the world's ways. The *outcome* of our acts is independent of our thoughts and desires. (The library is not closed because the sign *says* closed but because the door is locked, the staff has gone home, and so on.) If I believe the way is clear but a plate of glass stands in the way, I will experience the rude shock of a collision—like it or not. This sort of thing involved in the consequences of our belief-geared actions—potentially including pain, dismay, and disappointment—is the very paradigm of a *given*. And it is this sort of "given" that provides the quality-control monitor over our beliefs, and, even more critically, the methods and procedures by which our beliefs are established.

To be sure, *such* givens themselves are not cognitive, not world-descriptively informative facts. They lie in the affective order of the positive and the negative, not in the cognitive order of the informatively true or false. The pair of imparted developments, the distress of plans gone wrong, and the dismay of disappointed expectations are the sorts of shocks and negativities that are "given" to us when our beliefs do not jive with the world's ways—and such negative results are the sorts of belief-independent givens that provide a quality-control monitor on the processes and methods by which our beliefs are established. But even when our beliefs are provided by the sorts of methods from which the course of experience speaks, the question remains: are they really *true*?

The proper response at this point is to have resort to the concept of estimation. For while we cannot claim dogmatically that our methodology-validated beliefs are flat-out true, we can indeed claim that they afford our best-available *estimates* of the truth. And at this point there is no room for further complaint. For this sort of thing is in fact the best that we can do in the circumstances. And at *that* point it makes no moral or rational sense to complain that the best we can possibly do is not good enough. Requesting more than what is possible in the circumstances is inherently absurd.

The Evolutionary Aspect

The appeal to experience that is presently at issue involves a long story. Let us try to make it brief. The ancients saw man as "the rational animal" (*zoōn logon echōn*), set apart from the world's other creatures by the capacity for speech and deliberation. And following the precedent of Greek philosophy, Western thinkers have generally deemed the deliberate use of knowledge for the guidance of our actions to be at once the glory and the duty of *Homo sapiens*.

Humans have evolved within nature to fill the ecological niche of an intelligent being. Reason-deploying intelligence—the use of our brains to guide action by figuring out the apparent best—is the survival instrument of our species in much the same way that other creatures ensure their survival by being prolific, tough, or well-sheltered. Intelligence constitutes our particular "competitive advantage" in the evolutionary scheme of things. As Darwin himself already stressed, in a competitive Darwinian world an intelligent creature that can understand how things work in its environment and exploit this understanding through action thereby secures an evolutionary edge. And this means that practical reason—with its insistence on the intelligence in our quest for efficiency and effectiveness in satisfying our needs and wants—is an indispensable instrumentality programmed by evolution into the nature of the human condition.

Given the reasonable agent's well-advised predilection for *success* in one's ventures, the fact that the cognitive methods we employ have a good record of demonstrated effectiveness in regard to explanation, prediction, and control is not surprising but only to be expected: the community of rational inquirers would have given them up long ago were they not comparatively successful. The effectiveness of our cognitive methodology is thus readily accounted for on evolutionary principles that pivot on rational selection and the requirements for survival through adoption and transmission. Our possession of intelligence proceeds through *natural* selection, but our modus operandi in its employment proceeds through *rational* selection. So on both sides alike—the biological and the cultural—the pressures of evolutionary survival speak in favor of the rational economy that lies at the root of reason at large.

Our cognitive faculties are doubtless the product of *biological* evolution, but the processes and procedures by which we put them to work are the results of a *cultural* evolution that proceeds through rationally guided trial and error in circumstances of a pragmatic preference for retaining those processes and procedures that prove theorists efficient and effective. Thus, while biological evolution is doubtless based on Darwinian chance, cultural evolution has an aspect of Larmakian finalism. For a community of rational beings is more likely to select for cross-generational transmission those procedures, methods, and processes that are actually effective in realizing the goals at issue— at meeting their needs and desiderata. Rational people strongly favor what works. And progress in this direction is swift because once rationality gains an inch, it wants a mile. Of course, cultural evolution is shaped and canalized by constraints that themselves are the products of biological evolution. For our instincts, inclinations, and natural dispositions are all programmed into us by evolution. But then, too, it lies in the definitive nature of rationality to endorse those practices within the range of discernibly available alternatives that, as best we can tell, are comparatively optimal (on the basis of their cost-effectiveness) in realizing the objectives of the enterprise at issue. And it lies in the definitive makeup of rational beings that they will set for themselves aims and objectives that either are just or are somehow rooted in their needs (individually or collectively). And when one is dealing with intelligent beings—beings who govern their actions by their rationally forced beliefs about matters of fact and value—there is going to be a selective pressure (albeit one of rational rather than natural selection) on behalf of those cognitive methods that yield results that are, as best as one can tell, true, which is to say, those whose results succeed in the canalization of expectation (that is, in matters of prediction) and in the canalization of action (that is, in matters of application).

Yet people are surely not all that rational—they have their moments of aberration and self-indulgence. Might not such tendencies selectively favor the survival of the ineffective over the effective, of the fallacious rather than the true, and slant the process of cognitive evolution in inappropriate directions? C. S. Peirce certainly recognized this prospect: "Logicality in regard to practical matters . . . is the most useful quality an animal can possess, and might, therefore, result from the action of natural selection; but outside of these it is probably of more advantage to the animal to have his mind filled with pleasing and encouraging visions, independently of their truth; and thus, upon unpractical subjects, natural selection might occasion a fallacious tendency of thought."[3] However, the methodological orientation of the approach envisioned here provides a safeguard against an unwarranted penchant for such fallacious tendencies. At the level of individual beliefs "pleasing and encouraging visions" might indeed receive a survival-favoring impetus. But this unhappy prospect is effectively removed where a *systematic* method of inquiry is concerned—a method that must by its very synoptic nature lie in the sphere of the pragmatically effective.

Examples of the operation of evolutionary processes in the cognitive domain are not hard to come by. The intellectual landscape of human history is littered with the skeletal remains of the extinct dinosaurs of this sphere. Examples of such defunct methods for the acquisition and explanatory utilization of information include astrology, numerology, oracles, dream interpretation, the reading of tea leaves or bird entrails, animism, and the teleological physics of the Presocratics. No doubt, such processes continue operative in some human communities to this very day but not among those dedicated to serious inquiry into nature's ways—that is, scientists. There is nothing intrinsically absurd or inherently contemptible about such unorthodox cognitive programs; even the most occult of them have a long and not wholly unsuccessful history. (Think, for example, of the prominent role of numerological explanation beginning with Pythagoreanism in classical antiquity and moving on through Platonism and the medieval Arabs, down to Kepler in the Renaissance.) Distinctly different scientific methodologies and programs have been mooted: Ptolemaic "saving the phenomena" versus the hypothetico-deductive method, or, again, Baconian collectionism versus the post-Newtonian theory of experimental science. The emergence, development, and ultimate triumph of the scientific method of inquiry and explanation invite an evolutionary account—though clearly one that involves rational rather than natural selection.

An individual's heritage comes from two main sources: a biological heritage derived from the parents and a cultural heritage derived from the society. In the development of our knowledge it is our cultural heritage that becomes critical. To establish and perpetuate itself in any community of *rational* agents, a practice or method of procedure must prove itself in the course of experience. Not only must it be to some extent effective in realizing the pertinent aims and ends; it must also prove itself to be more efficient than comparably available alternatives. With societies composed of rational agents, the pressure of means-ends efficacy is ever at work in forging a process of cultural (rather than natural) selection for replacing less by more cost-effective ways of achieving the group's committed ends—its cognitive ends emphatically included.

The Rationale of Rationality

This said, it must nevertheless be acknowledged that the linkage of rational appropriateness to successful practice is not airtight. Our most rational plans and decisions "gang aft agley."

Reason can issue no absolute guarantees. We neither have nor can secure any categorical assurance that doing what reason urges will turn out to be the best thing to have done, that reason's recommendations may not actually prove counterproductive. And this means that we must live the life of reason in the full recognition that, while always and everywhere insisting on obedience to its requirements, it nevertheless cannot guarantee that in following its counsels as best we can, we may not actually damage rather than enhance the prospects of attaining our legitimate ends. Reason recognizes that there is no way of averting the fact that life in this world is a risky proposition. In epistemic matters, as elsewhere, it asks no more of us (but also no less!) than that we do the best we can in the circumstances.

Why then honor reason's demands—why follow its guidance? Simply because abstract analysis and concrete experience alike indicate that we can do no better. There is, and can be, no somehow superior reason-variant course of procedure, for, after all, if any seemingly "other" course of action boded a better prospect of success, then rationality itself would at once mandate its adoption. Fractious creatures though we humans are, evolution—biological and cultural alike—has programmed in us a tendency to respect the voice of reason. And if and when we do actually listen to that voice, we hear its insistence that by all visible indications no more promising source of counsel is available to us.

To be sure, we are creatures of free will, as free to choose the course of unreason as that of reason, of foolishness as that of wisdom. But here, as everywhere else in life, choice comes at a price. The price that unreason exacts from us is a diminution of the prospect of obtaining those results whose realization is in our best interests, realistically construed. Both theoretical reflection and evolutionary science combine to indicate that the most powerful case for cognitive rationality is that based on its practical utility.

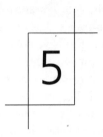

Specificity Prioritization and the Primacy of the Particular

Specificity Prioritization

The story is told that Herbert Spencer said of Thomas Buckle (or was it the other way around, as it could just as well have been) that his idea of a tragedy was a beautiful theory destroyed by a recalcitrant fact. A fundamental epistemic principle is at issue here, namely, that when the limited particularity of fact and the broad generality of theory come into conflict in the case of otherwise plausible propositions, then it is the fact that will prevail. Facts, as the proverb has it, are stubborn things: facts must prevail over theories, observations over speculations, concrete instances over abstract generalities, limited laws over broad hypotheses. When other things are anything like equal, specificity predominates over generality in matters of fact.

And so a far-reaching *principle of specificity precedence* comes into view. In cases of conflict or contradiction in our information, the cognitive dissonance that needs to be removed is to be resolved in favor of the more particularly concrete, definite party to the conflict. The more general, the more cases included, the more open to error: generality is a source of vulnerability, and when clashes arise, particularity enjoys priority. We have to presume that specifics are in better probative condition than generalities because they are by nature easier to evidentiate, seeing that generalities encompass a multitude of specifics. In contrast, seemingly established generalities are easier to disestablish than specifics because a single counterinstance among many possibilities will disestablish a generality, whereas it takes something definite and case specific to disestablish a particularity. Accordingly, it transpires that ordinarily and in "normal" circumstances specificities are on safer ground and thereby enjoy probative precedence in situations of discord and inconsistency. When mere information is being distilled into coherent knowledge, specificity prioritization is the rule.

Some Illustrations of the Principle

Such a *principle of specificity precedence* can be illustrated from many different points of view. As already noted, it is a standard feature of scientific practice that when theory and observation clash, it is, in general, observation that prevails.[1] The practice of monitoring hypothetical theorizing by means of experimentation is characteristic of the scientific process, and the *principle of specificity precedence* is fundamental here. Throughout, whenever speculation clashes with the phenomena, a conjectured hypotheses with the data at our disposal, or a theory with observation, then it is generally—and almost automatically—the former that is made to give way. That is, presumption stands on the side of specificity throughout the realm of factual inquiry.

This circumstance obtains not only in clashes between observation with theory but also in clashes between a lower level (less general or abstract) theory and one that is of a higher (more general and abstract) level. Here, too, the comparatively specific rival will prevail in situations of conflict. And the general principle prevails with the historical sciences every bit as much as with the natural sciences. A single piece of new textual evidence or a single item of new archaeological discovery can suffice to call a conflicting theory into question. Here, too, a penchant for specificity preference is very much in operation.

Philosophy affords yet another illustration of specificity preference. The work of Thomas Reid (1710–1796) and the philosophers of the Scottish School illustrates this in an especially vivid way. These thinkers reasoned as follows: Suppose a conflict arises between some speculative teaching or philosophical theorizing and certain more particular, down-to-earth, bits of everyday common sense. Then it, of course, will and must be those philosophical contentions that must give way.

In this spirit Reid insisted that common sense must prevail over the more speculative teaching of philosophy. Maintaining that most philosophers themselves have some sense of this he observes wryly that "it is pleasant to observe the fruitless pains which Bishop Berkeley took to show that his system . . . did not contradict the sentiment of the vulgar, but only those of the philosophers."[2] Reid firmly held that any clash between philosophy and common sense must be resolved in the latter's favor. Should such a clash occur, "The philosopher himself must yield . . . [because] such [commonsense] principles are older, and of more authority, than philosophy; she rests upon them as her basis, not they upon her. If she could overturn them she would become buried in their ruins, but all the engines of philosophical subtlety are too weak for this purpose."[3] In any conflict between philosophy and everyday commonsense beliefs it is the latter that must prevail. The down-to-earth lessons of ordinary experience must always take precedence over any conflicting speculations of philosophical theorizing. On this point the Scottish common-sensists were emphatic. And in fact most metaphilosophical accounts of philosophizing have agreed with this specificity-favoring point of view.

Yet another illustration of specificity preference comes, perhaps surprisingly, from pure mathematics. In deliberating about the relationship between mathematics proper and metamathematical theorizing about mathematical issues, the great German mathematician David Hilbert (1862–1943) also argued for specificity preference. If any conflict should arise between substantive mathematical findings and large-scale metamathematical theory, then it is, so he maintained, automatically the latter that must yield by way of abandonment or modification. Here, too, we are to favor concrete specificity over abstract generality, seeing that, across a wide range of mathematics, abstract metamathematical theories are comparatively more risky. Accordingly, consider what Arthur Fine calls "Hilbert's Maxim," namely, the thesis that "Metatheoretic arguments [about a theory] must satisfy more stringent requirements [of acceptability] than those placed on the arguments used by the theory in question."[4] So the mathematical realm can afford yet another illustration of specificity preference. Throughout our inquiry into the reality of things, it appears that our pursuit of knowledge prioritizes specificity. That is, presumption stands on the side of comparative specificity and definiteness.

The Question of Rationale

Is there a cogent rationale for this? Are there sound reasons of general principle why specificity should be advantaged? An affirmative answer is clearly in order here. The reasoning at issue runs somewhat as follows. Consider a conflict case of the sort that now concerns us. Here, in the presence of various other uncontested "innocent by-standers" (x), we are forced to choose between a generality (g) and a specificity (s) because a situation of the following generic structure obtains:

$(g \& x) \rightarrow {\sim}s$ or equivalently $(s \& x) \rightarrow {\sim}g$

It is clear, here, that with the unproblematic context x fixed in place either s or g must be sacrificed. But since g, being general, encompasses a whole variety of other special cases—some of which might well also go wrong—we have, in effect, a forced choice occasioned by a clash between a many-case manifold and the fewer-case competitor. And since the extensiveness of the former affords a greater scope for error, the latter is bound to be the safer bet. As a rule, generalities are more vulnerable than specificities. When other things are anything like equal, it is clearly easier for error to gain entry into a larger than into a smaller manifold of claims.

To be sure, it deserves to be noted that what is basically at issue with specificity preference is not a propositional truth claim but a procedural principle of presumption. What is at issue is not a factual gen-

eralization to the effect that specificities inevitably prevail over generalities but a precept of epistemic practice on the order of "believe the
testimony of your own eyes" or "accept the claim for which the available evidence is stronger." It is a matter of the procedural principle.
And, of course, one can go wrong here: It is not true that what your
eyes tell you is always so or that the truth always lies on the side of the
stronger evidential case in hand. All that we have—and all that is at issue—is that such methodological precepts of rational procedure indicate a process that will generally lead us aright. Though not infalli-
ble, they are good guides to practice. Such a principle of practice
reflects a matter of general adequacy rather than foolproof correctness. And the justification at issue is thus one of functional efficacy, of
effectively serving the purposes of the practice at issue. Here, as elsewhere, presumption is less a matter of demonstrating a universal truth
than of validating a modus operandi on the basis of its general efficacy.

A Curious Inversion: The Case of Counterfactuals

It is, however, necessary to come to terms with the striking circumstance that there is an important family of cases where more usual presumption of specificity prioritization is in fact inverted and the
reverse process of a generality prioritization obtains. This occurs when
we are dealing not with matters of fact, but with fact-contradicting assumptions and hypotheses.[5]
By way of illustration, consider the counterfactual conditional:
If he had been born in 1999, then Julius Caesar would not have
died in 44 B.C. but would be a mere infant in 2001.

This arises in the context of the following issue-salient beliefs:
1. Julius Caesar was born in 100 B.C.
2. Julius Caesar is long dead, having died at the age of fifty-six in
44 B.C.
3. Julius Caesar was not born in 1999 A.D.
4. Anyone born in 1999 A.D. will only be an infant by 2001.
5. People cannot die before they are born.

And let us now introduce the supposition of not-(3) via the following:
Assumption: Suppose that not-(3), that is, Julius Caesar was born in 1999 A.D.

In the face of this assumption we must, of course, follow its explicit instruction to dismiss (1) and (3). Thesis (4) is safe and inherent in the very definition of infancy. But even with these adjustments, inconsistency remains and confronts us with two distinct acceptance/rejection alternatives:

(2), (4)/(1), (3), (5)
(4), (5)/(1), (2), (3)

In effect we are now constrained to a choice between the specific (2) on the one hand and the general (5) on the other. At this point, however, the "natural" resolution afforded by the *principle of generality precedence* that holds in these purely hypothetical cases will prioritize the more general and instance-encompassing (5) over the case-specific (2), thereby eliminating that first alternative. With not-(1) fixed by hypothesis, the conclusion of the initial counterfactual then at once follows from (4) and (5). In effect, that counterfactual is the product of generality prioritization. The perplexity of an unnatural counterfactual along the lines of "If Julius Cesar had been born in 1999, then he would have been born again from the dead" would be averted.

As this example illustrates, *in deliberating with respect to fact-contradicting assumptions, generality precedence comes into play.* And this betokens a larger lesson. In determining which beliefs should give way in the face of counterfactual assumptions, we should let informativeness be our guide, so that authentic generality is now in the driver's seat.[6] Rational procedure in speculative contexts becomes a matter of keeping our systemic grip on the manifold of relevant information as best we can.

Consider another example:
If this rubber band were made of copper, what then?

This question arises in an epistemic context where the following beliefs are salient:

1. This band is made of rubber.
2. This band is not made of copper.
3. This band does not conduct electricity.
4. Things made of rubber do not conduct electricity.
5. Things made of copper do conduct electricity.

Let it be that we are now instructed to accept the hypothesis
   Not-(2): This band is made of copper.
Then the following two propositional sets are the hypothesis-compatible maximal consistent subsets of our specified belief-set B:

   {(3), (4)}   corresponding to the acceptance/rejection
                       alternative (3), (4)/(1), (2), (5)
   {(4), (5)}   corresponding to the acceptance/rejection
                       alternative (4), (5)/(1), (2), (3)

The first alternative corresponds to the counterfactual
   If this band were made of copper, then copper would not conduct
   electricity (since this band does not conduct electricity).

The second alternative corresponds to the counterfactual
   If this band were made of copper, then it would conduct electricity (since copper conducts electricity).

In effect we are driven to a choice between (3) and (5), that is, between a particular feature of this band and a general fact about copper things. However, its greater generality qualifies (5) as being systemically more informative, and its prioritization is therefore appropriate. Accordingly, we will retain (4) and (5) along with not-(2), and therefore accept that second counterfactual as appropriate. And this exemplifies a general situation of generality preference in matters of counterfactual reasoning.

Natural versus Unnatural Counterfactuals

The distinction between "natural" and "unnatural" counterfactuals is, of course, crucial in the present context. To illustrate this, let us suppose that we know that all the coins in the till are made of copper. Then we can say without hesitation:

If the coin I have in mind is in the till, then it is made of copper.

But we certainly cannot say counterfactually:

If the coin I have in mind were in the till, then it would be made of copper.

After all, I could perfectly well have a certain silver coin in mind, which would certainly not change its composition by being placed in the till.

But just how is the difference between the two cases to be explained?

Let $C = \{c_1, c_2, \ldots, c_n\}$ be the set of coins in the till, where by hypothesis all of these c_i are made of copper.

And now consider the assumption:

Let x be one of the c_i (that is, let it be some otherwise unspecified one of those coins presently in the till).

Clearly this assumption, together with our given, "All of the c_i are made of copper," will entail "x is made of copper" so that the first conditional is validated.

But in the second case we merely have the assumption:

Let x be a coin in the till (though not necessarily one of those presently there).

Now, of course, this hypothesis joined to "All of the coins presently in the till are made of copper" will obviously not yield that conclusion. Accordingly, the second counterfactual is in trouble, since the information available to serve as its enthymematic basis is insufficient to validate the requisite deduction. The two conditionals are different because they involve different assumptions of differing epistemic status, a difference subtly marked by use of the indicative in the first case and the subjunctive in the second. For in the former case we are dealing merely with de facto arrangements, whereas in the latter with a lawful generalization. And so generality prioritization speaks for the latter alternative. Lawfulness makes all the difference here.

Consider the question, "What if Booth had not murdered Lincoln?" And let us suppose that the salient beliefs here stand as follows:

1. Lincoln was murdered in April 1865.
2. Murder is deliberate killing, so given that Lincoln was murdered, it was by someone deliberately trying to kill him.
3. Booth murdered Lincoln.
4. Only Booth was deliberately trying to kill Lincoln in April 1865.

Observe that (1), (2), (4) $\vdash$ (3). Now suppose that not-(3). Then we must abandon one of the trio: (1), (2), (4). Here (2) is a definitional truth. And (4) is a general fact, whereas (1) is but a matter of specific fact. So now the rule of precedence for matters of generality/informativeness marks (1) as the weakest link and we arrive at

If Booth had not murdered Lincoln, Lincoln would not have been murdered in April 1865.

In a similar vein, we have the problem of explaining how it is that the subjunctively articulated counterfactual,

If Oswald had not shot Kennedy, then nobody would have,

seems perfectly acceptable, whereas the corresponding indicative conditional,

If Oswald did not shoot Kennedy, then no one did,

seems deeply problematic.[7] And within the presently contemplated frame of reference the answer is straightforward. The background of accepted belief here is as follows:

1. Kennedy was shot.
2. Oswald shot Kennedy.
3. Oswald acted alone: No one apart from Oswald was trying to shoot Kennedy.

Now suppose that (2) is replaced by its negation not-(2), that is, that Oswald had not shot Kennedy. For the sake of consistency we are then required to abandon either (1) or (3). The informativeness-geared policy of presumption via generality precedence in matters of mere hypothesis now rules in favor of retaining (3), thus dropping (1) and arriving at the former of that pair of conditionals. The alternative but inappropriate step of dismissing (1) would, by contrast, issue in that second, decidedly implausible counterfactual. To be sure, this conditional could in theory be recast in a more complex form that would rescue it:

> If Oswald did not shoot Kennedy, then no one did, so since Kennedy was shot, Oswald did it.

In this revised version the conditional in effect constitutes a *reductio ad absurdum* of the idea that Oswald did not shoot Kennedy. But it is now clear that these conditionals address very different questions, namely, the (1)-rejecting

> What if Oswald had not shot Kennedy?

and the (1)-retaining

> Who shot Kennedy?

The Key Lesson

What is thus crucial with counterfactuals is the determination of precedence and priority in a consistency-restoring right-of-way allocation in cases of conflict. We proceed here on the basis of the rule that

> In counterfactual reasoning, the right-of-way priority among the issue-salient beliefs is determined in terms of their generality of import by way of informativeness in the systemic context at hand.

The situation can be summarized in the unifying slogan that in hypothetical situations the standard modus operandi of presumption prioritizes beliefs on the basis of *systematicity preference.* But this matter of right-of-way is now determined with reference to informativeness within the wider context of our knowledge. When we play fast and loose with the world's facts, we need the security of keeping its fundamentals in place. In particular, it is standard policy that *in counter-factual contexts, propositions viewed as comparatively more informative in the systemic context at hand will take priority over those that are less so.* While revisions by way of curtailment and abandonment in our family of relevant belief are unavoidable and inevitable in the face of belief-countervailing hypotheses, we want to give up as little as possible. And here the ruling principle is, "Break the chain of inconsistency at its weakest link in point of systemic informativeness."

In counterfactual contexts, generalities accordingly take precedence over specificities. Once we enter the realm of fact-contravening hypotheses those general theses and themes that we subordinate to specifics in factual matters now become our life preservers. We cling to them for dear life and do all that is necessary to keep them in place. "Salvage as much information about the actual condition of things as you possibly can" is now our watchword. Accordingly, specifics and particularities will here yield to generalizations and abstractions. And so in determining which beliefs are to give way in the face of counter-factual assumptions we do and should let informativeness be our guide. Keeping our systemic grip on the manifold of relevant information is the crux and speaks clearly for generality-precedence here.

Conclusion

The preceding line of thought reinforces a point for which the present author has argued for many years, namely, that lawfulness (in the laws-of-nature sense of the term) and generality of range are pivotal features in the treatment of counterfactuals.[8] Once we enter the realm of fact-contravening hypothesis and suppositions, then those general truths and theories become our sheet armor, so that specifics and particularities now yield way to generalizations and abstractions. The overall lesson then is clear. When a clash among seemingly acceptable propositions occurs in *factual* contexts, considerations of evidential plausibility lead us to adopt the stance of specificity preference. But in counterfactual contexts where the economics of information conservation is paramount, our deliberations must pivot the generality preference at issue with systemic cogency.

To be sure, in the case of a counterfactual supposition that is itself particular we may have to make a generalization give way to it. This arises standardly in the case of thought experiments contemplating outcomes that may defeat generalizations. Thus consider the following counterfactual relating to testing the generalization (g) that heavy objects (like rocks) fall to earth when released:

> If this heavy rock had not fallen to earth when it was released at altitude yesterday, then generalization g would be false.

Here we have the following beliefs about the situation:
1. A heavy rock was released at altitude yesterday.
2. The rock then fell to earth.
3. Heavy objects (like rocks) fall to earth when released at altitude (= generalization g).

When now instructed to assume not-(2), the resulting inconsistency forces a choice between abandoning the specific (1) and the general (3). With automatic generality precedence, one would be constrained to retain (3) and jettison (1). But that, of course, is not how things work in such a thought experiment. For now the particular thesis at issue, namely (1), is here immunized against rejection by the fact of its constituting part of the very hypothesis at issue.

* * *

The lesson of these deliberations is clear. In matters of conflict within the factual domain, presumption lies on the side of specificity, whereas in the speculatively counterfactual domain it favors lawful generality. In the larger scheme of things, two diametrically opposed principles—specificity prioritization and generality prioritization—are in operation in our overall deliberations. But they obtain in very different sectors of the cognitive terrain, namely, factual inquiry and counterfactual speculation. And, in both cases alike, it is the purposive nature of the enterprise that determines the appropriateness of the correlative prioritization principle. Here, it is not form but matter that follows function.

The purposive manifold of the particular area of deliberation at issue is the determinative factor. With factual inquiry we aim at the security of our cognitive commitments and accordingly opt for specificity as the more reliable guide. By contrast, with counterfactual reasonings we look for the results of disbelieved hypotheses and strive to retain the maximum of information that survives the turmoil produced in our cognitive commitments by the impact of discordant assumptions. And here, as elsewhere, it is the difference in the aims and purposes of the enterprise at hand that accounts for the procedural process that is appropriate.

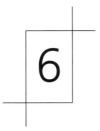

6

Dismissing Extremely
Remote Possibilities

Introduction

In its details, the relationship between theoretical and practical reason is complex and convoluted. For as philosophers have long recognized and emphasized there are significant differences between theoretical and practical rationality, between proceeding rationally in solving purely theoretical problems (where nothing save the possibility of mistaken beliefs is at risk) and so proceeding in resolving practical issues (where actual harm of some sort might be incurred). There is, however, no more striking illustration of this situation than the little heeded issue of the treatment of remote possibilities—those whose probability is *extremely* small. The prime question that arises here is this: In rational decision making, should a diminutive probability (one of an infinitesimal magnitude ϵ) be seen as being indistinguishable from 0 and thus effectively treated as something that has no magnitude at all? In deploying diminutive probabilities in the course of using expected-value comparisons as guides for decision making, could and should we adopt the equation $\epsilon = 0$? Or is it inappropriate to neglect even "negligibly small" quantities here?

Effectively Zero Probabilities

A probability has to be a quantity between 0 and 1. Now, numbers between 0 and 1 can get to be very small indeed: As N gets bigger, $1/N$ will become insignificantly minute. What, then, are we to do about extremely small probabilities in the rational management of risks?[1]

On this issue there is a systemic disagreement between probabilists working on theory-oriented issues in mathematics or natural science and decision theorists who address practical decision-oriented issues related to human affairs. The former take the line that small numbers are small numbers and must be taken into account as such—that is, as the small quantities they actually are. The latter tend to take the view that small probabilities represent extremely remote prospects and can be written off. (*De minimis non curat lex,* as the old legal precept has it: in effect, in human affairs there is no need to bother with trifles.) When something is about as probable as a thousand fair coins when tossed a thousand times coming up heads, then, so it is held, we can pretty well forget about it as worthy of concern. As a matter of practical policy we operate with probabilities on the principle that when $x \le \epsilon$, then $x = 0$. We can defensibly take the line that in our human dealings in real-life situations a sufficiently remote possibility can—for all sensible purposes—be viewed as being of probability 0.[2]

Accordingly, such remote possibilities can simply be dismissed, and the outcomes with which they are associated can accordingly be set aside. And in "the real world" people do in fact seem to be prepared to treat minute probabilities as effectively 0, taking certain sufficiently improbable eventualities as no longer representing *real* possibilities. As one writer on insurance puts it, "People . . . refuse to worry about losses whose probability is below some [small] threshold. Probabilities below the threshold are treated as though they were zero."[3] To be sure, remotely possible events *can* occur in some sense of the term, but *can* is now functioning in a figurative sense: it is no longer seen as denoting a realistic prospect.

In purely epistemic contexts, as David Lewis has pointed out, the assignment of probability 0 or 1 indicates "absolute certainty [that] is tantamount to a firm resolution never to change your mind, no matter what."[4] However, when using decision theory in the context of choosing a course of action, setting a probability at 0 works quite differently. For it now means no more than ruling out the corresponding possibility for the practical purposes of a particular case, dismissing it as an object of appropriate concern in the situation at hand.[5] The significance of such a probability-annihilation is thus something rather different in these two contexts of deliberation.

To be sure, it needs to be stressed that in practical contexts such a treatment of the probabilities at issue is essentially a matter of fiat, and of resolving that as a matter of policy a certain level of sufficiently low probability can be taken as a threshold below which we are no longer dealing with "*real* possibilities" and with "*genuine* risks." Such remote eventualities are taken to merit being dismissed "for all practical purposes." This recourse to effective zerohood does not, of course, represent a strictly objective, factual circumstance. (After all, $\in\ =0$ is a literal falsehood.) It reflects a matter of choice or decision, namely, the *practical* step of treating certain theoretically extant possibilities as unreal, as not worth bothering about, as being literally *negligible* and meriting being set at 0. It is not that those minimalities do not exist, but that we cease to trouble ourselves with them because of the improbability of matters going wrong. We simply dismiss them from the range of practical concern.

The thesis $\in\ =0$ is not being adopted as a factual contention. It is a matter of a *practical policy* of procedure. The situation is akin to that of statements like "In the absence of specific counterindications, accept what people say as true." Taken as a thesis of literal fact (with the word *is* replacing *accept as*) the claim is false. But it could, nevertheless, prove to be useful and productive as a principle of practice.

How Small Is Small Enough?

Of course, the question remains: How small is small enough for being "effectively 0"? With what value of $\in$ does $\in\ =0$ begin: just exactly where does the threshold of effective zerohood lie?

This is clearly not something that can be decided once and for all. The threshold may vary from case to case and possibly even from individual to individual, changing with the "cautiousness" of the person involved, representing an aspect of an individual's stance toward the whole risk-taking process. And it may also be taken to vary with the magnitude of the stake at issue. For it seems plausible to allow the threshold of effective zerohood to reflect the magnitude of the threat at issue, taking lower values as the magnitude of the stake at issue increases. (Such a policy seems in smooth accord with the fundamental principle of risk management that greater potential losses should be risked only when their chances for realization are less.)

The empirical facts seem to indicate that in deliberating about risks to human life, for example, there is some tendency to take as a baseline a person's chance of death by natural disasters (or "acts of God"), roughly one in a million each year in the United States. This would be seen as something akin to the "noise level" of a physical system, and fatality probabilities significantly smaller than this would thus be seen as negligible. Such an approach seems to underlay the Food and Drug Administration's proposed conservative standard of "one in 1 million over a lifetime."[6] People's stance in the face of the probability that when embarking on a commercial airplane trip they will end up as an aviation fatality (which stood at roughly one in 300 million in the United States prior to September 11, 2001) also illustrates this perspective. (Most people neither worry nor insure unless "the company pays.")

To be sure, one important point must be noted in this connection. The probability values that we treat as effectively 0 must be values of which, in themselves, we are very sure indeed. And real-life probability values are seldom all that precise. Accordingly, there will in general be considerable difficulty in sustaining the judgment that a certain probability is indeed effectively 0. A striking instance is afforded by the Atomic Energy Commission–sponsored "Rasmussen Report" of the 1970s (named after Norman C. Rasmussen, the study director) on the accident risks of nuclear power plants:

> From the viewpoint of a person living in the general vicinity of a reactor, the likelihood of being killed in any one year in a reactor accident is one chance in 300,000,000 and the likelihood

of being injured in any one year in a reactor accident is one chance in 150,000,000.[7]

The theoretical calculations that sustain such a finding invoke so many assumptions regarding facts, circumstances, and operating principles that such probability estimates are extremely shaky. Outside the domain of purely theoretical science, we are too readily plunged below the threshold of experimental error and will thus confront great difficulties in supporting minute probability distinctions in the sphere of technological and social applications. Statistical probabilities can be very problematic in this regard, particularly since statistical data are often flawed or, in the case of very rare events, not available. Personal probabilities—that is, mere guesses—are also very vulnerable in this context of assessing very low probabilities. (For example, the flood victims the geographer R. W. Kates interviewed flatly denied that flood could ever recur in their area, erroneously attributing previous floods to freak combinations of circumstances that were extremely unlikely to reoccur.[8]) One writer has maintained that in safety-engineering contexts it simply is not possible to construct sufficiently convincing arguments to support very small probabilities (below 10^5).[9] Moreover, it is sometimes tempting to exaggerate the extent to which a distinct possibility is remote. And indeed a diversified literature has been devoted to describing the ways in which the estimation of very low probabilities can go astray.[10] So there is ample room for due caution in this regard.

Why Accept a Threshold of "Effective Zerohood"?

In seeing subliminal probabilities as negligible, and thereby treating those infinitesimal quantities as effectively nil, we set a threshold beneath which those diminutive probabilities can be set at 0. But why adopt such a probability threshold—why treat sufficiently remote hazards as simply "unreal?" What justifies this bit of seeming unrealism?

The idea of treating very small probabilities as effectively 0 goes back a long way—to Buffon in the seventeenth century and Cournot in the eighteenth.[11] This stratagem treats certain eventuations as *moral* impossibilities and their nonrealization as *moral* certainties (in the traditional terminology, for which one might substitute the designation of *practical*). The original motivation for adopting a threshold of effective zerohood arose out of Daniel Bernoulli's "St. Petersburg paradox" arising via the following imaginary game:[12]

> A fair coin is to be tossed until a head appears. If it does so on the nth toss, the gambler is then to be paid 2^n ducats. How much should the gambler be prepared to pay to enter the game?

It is easy to see that the mathematical expectation of this gamble is

$$\sum_{n=1}^{\infty} (2^n) \times (1/2)^n$$

which is clearly infinite. So by the usual standards the gambler should be willing to pay any finite stake, however large. This is clearly counterintuitive. Buffon proposed to resolve this problem by emphasizing that the probability $(1/2)^n$ soon becomes very small indeed for increasing n. Once the stage is reached where these small-probability eventuations are seen as "effectively impossible," the mathematical expectation of return becomes finite, and the paradox is resolved.

There are, to be sure, other and perhaps better ways of overcoming this particular obstacle.[13] But this classic paradox is not the only reason for dismissing remote possibilities. Yet another reason for dismissing subliminally improbable possibilities is that there are just too many of them to cope with in practical terms. To be asked to reckon with such remote possibilities is to baffle our thought by sending it on a chase after endless alternatives. And there are yet more pressing reasons for dismissing sufficiently improbable possibilities. This lies in our need and desire to avoid stultifying action. It is simply "human nature" to dismiss sufficiently remote eventualities in one's personal calculations.

The "vacationer's dilemma" of display 1 illustrates this phenomenon. Only by dismissing certain sufficiently remote catastrophic misfortunes as lying outside the range of *real* possibilities—thus treating them as negligible—can one avoid the stultification of action on anything like the standard decision-making approach represented by expected-value calculations. The vacationer takes the plausible line of viewing the chance of disaster as effectively 0, thereby eliminating that unacceptable possible outcome from playing a role by way of intimidation. People generally (and justifiably) proceed on the assumption that the probability of sufficiently unlikely disasters can be set at 0; that in certain common life contexts unpleasant eventuations of extreme improbability can be dismissed as lying outside the realm of "real" or "practical" possibilities. Worrying about extremely remote possibilities—even of quite substantial disasters—simply makes life too difficult.[14] So, here, fitness considerations seem to favor the dismissal of extremely remote possibilities, seeing that this enables us to keep our practice within the framework of expectation-based decision theory without having to take anomalous and counterintuitive results in stride.

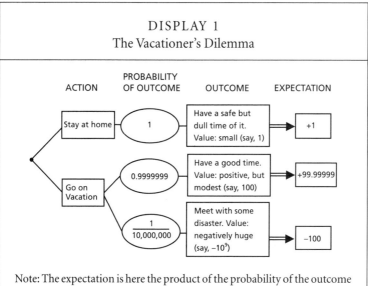

DISPLAY 1
The Vacationer's Dilemma

ACTION	PROBABILITY OF OUTCOME	OUTCOME	EXPECTATION
Stay at home	1	Have a safe but dull time of it. Value: small (say, 1)	+1
Go on Vacation	0.9999999	Have a good time. Value: positive, but modest (say, 100)	+99.99999
	$\frac{1}{10,000,000}$	Meet with some disaster. Value: negatively huge (say, -10^9)	−100

Note: The expectation is here the product of the probability of the outcome times its value. Thus, for the bottom line we have $10^{-7} \times -10^9 = -100$.

We thus see that the dismissal of extremely remote possibilities will in some cases have its advantages. For a reliance on the standard mechanisms of decision theory will in some circumstances no longer be sensible unless we are prepared to dismiss extremely small probabilities as 0.[15]

Without some such practical policy, mathematical expectation is no longer a safe and sensible guide to rational decision making in such probabilistically extreme situations.

To be sure, there are also cases in which we incur a disadvantage when we set $\in$ = 0. Thus, consider the situation of display 2, in which a person is confronted with the choice to pay fifty cents to enter a lottery with a one-in-a-million chance of winning $1 million or to abstain from this gamble. If the person enters, his expectation of gain is $1.00, so our subject would, on classical principles, be enjoined to enter the lottery. But if we adopted the idea of setting $\in$ = 0, then the expected value comparison will balance out at 0, so that on the basis of classical decision-making principles our agent would be entirely indifferent toward the alternatives.

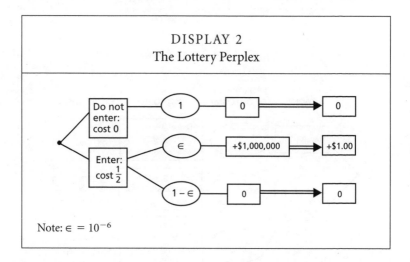

DISPLAY 2
The Lottery Perplex

Note: $\in$ = 10^{-6}

The policy of setting $\in$ at 0 looks rather different in the two contexts. In the case of the vacationer's dilemma it enables one to achieve an attractive benefit in the face of a vastly remote and improbable prospect of disaster. In the lottery perplex case it leads one to foregoing a palatable benefit. As a general policy it has its costs as well as its benefits. Just where does this leave us?

The Question of Validation

The very issue before us can itself be viewed in a decision-theoretic perspective. For in addressing such decision problems we implicitly also confront a second-order decision problem, namely, that of deciding whether to employ the policy R^+ of setting $\in = 0$ or to employ the policy R^- of not doing so. Proceeding at this point in the orthodox way, we make the expected-value calculation in both ways and then compare. Thus consider the situation of the vacationer's dilemma from the methodological standpoint, as in display 3. Viewed on this basis a comparison of the expected results indicates that the second alternative clearly looks better than the first on grounds of dominance, so that R^+ is in order.

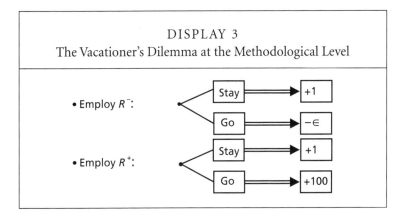

DISPLAY 3
The Vacationer's Dilemma at the Methodological Level

But by contrast consider the structure of the lottery perplex in display 4. Here the choice between R^- and R^+ is clearly indifferent: we are led to the same outcome either way.

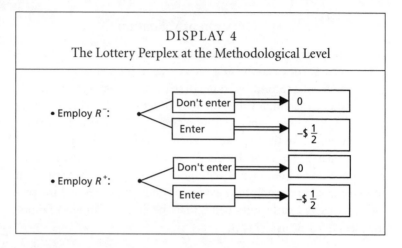

DISPLAY 4
The Lottery Perplex at the Methodological Level

The point is that the procedural issue of setting $\in$ at 0 can itself be seen as a second-order decision issue and addressed on this basis.

Overcoming a Problem

A further problem looms on the horizon—the so-called lottery paradox.[16] For the fact of it is that a substantial accumulation of minute chances can become significant.[17] Thus if we routinely take the step of setting $\in$ = 0 for diminutive $\in$, then consider a lottery with a zillion tickets, so that the probability that the outcome will lie in any given compartment is less than some diminutive $\in$. Then, on the one hand, we have

The probability that *some* ticket holder will win is one.

While, on the other hand, since chance for any given ticket holder is $\in$, which we now set at 0, we have it that since 0 × (anything) = 0, we are committing ourselves to

the probability that the outcome will be one of those tickets, 0 × (the number of tickets), that is, 0.

By repeating this reasoning once for each ticket, we reach the result that "the probability that the outcome will favor any one of those tickets is 0." And this is clearly at variance with our initial finding. Our policy of setting diminutive probabilities to 0 has plunged us into a contradiction. How are we to come to terms with this inconsistency? Perhaps the best step here is to take the line that equating ∈ with 0 is something we can indulge in only once within the overall decision-making context at issue.[18] To do this repeatedly would be a matter of having too much of a good thing. Here as elsewhere overindulgence can be the road to disaster. For a proposition claiming an outcome whose probability becomes 1 when we set ∈ = 0 will be said to be *virtually certain*. And, as the lottery paradox shows, a conjunction of such propositions may *or may not* itself turn out to be virtually certain.

Accordingly, we can now lay claim to the following principle of practical deliberation:

> *In contexts of practical reasoning—but here only, and not in purely cognitive matters—it is acceptable to include among the premisses one (but only one!) virtually certain proposition.*

It may seem odd to contemplate a rule of procedure that can be used only a limited number of times. But an analogy may help to make this restriction more plausible. Consider the rule of practice at issue in the following abbreviative convention: in writing omit every fourth letter (counting a space as a letter). Let us apply it to the sentence at the beginning of this section:

IT*MAY*SEEM*ODD*TO*CONTEMPLATE*A*RULE OF*PROCEDURE

In implementing that suppression rule one arrives at:

IT*AY*EEMODDTO*ONTMPLTE**RUEOFPROEDUE

Here it is (perhaps just) possible for a reasonably clever person to figure out what is being said. But it can be left as an exercise for the reader to verify that matters are reduced to a hopeless condition when the rule is applied twice over in dealing with the same text.

In just this way, the policy of setting $\epsilon = 0$ is something that must be employed not only with caution and discretion but also rarely. Indeed: *it is a practical device that one can afford to use only once in the course of addressing a given problem.* There are various useful and appropriate practices that can be stretched too far—practical resources whose *repeated* use may, rather than being helpful, work to defeat the purpose at hand. The dismissal of minute possibilities is simply yet another instance of this larger phenomenon.

Conclusion

As noted above, the lottery paradox shows that we cannot always and everywhere proceed on the somewhat delusional basis that $\epsilon = 0$. But this does not mean, of course, that we should not expect to get away with it in judiciously selected occasions. After all, we must not lose sight of the consideration that setting ϵ at 0 is not a theoretical fact but a practical resource. In life we have to take risks. And a ruling maxim of sensible procedure here is inherent in the following practical policy:

> *If proceeding x-wise is advantageous or convenient, and if doing so only very rarely leads to error or difficulty, then it is sensible and appropriate to proceed in this way in the absence of case-specific indications to the contrary.*

Setting ϵ at 0 falls under exactly this practical policy—indeed, it is something of a quintessential instance of its operation.

In the final analysis it needs to be acknowledged that there are three sorts of decision-making situations:
- *Normal situations,* in which we can employ the standard process of comparing expected values.
- *Catastrophe-threatening situations,* in which there are risks we just would not want to run no matter how small their probability.
- *Extremely remote probability situations,* in which we would choose to apply the improbability dismissive ($\epsilon = 0$) tactic discussed above.

The problem, of course, is deciding how to proceed when worst comes to worst, that is, when the situation we confront falls into *both* of the last two categories.

At this point we are best advised to step back from the decision question itself and view it in a different light, by asking yet another decision question at the higher level of process and procedure—namely, which of the alternative approaches available affords us the best choice in addressing the decision problem at hand? We are, in a manner of speaking, impelled to rise to the higher level of a second-order decision problem. And it is at exactly this stage that theoretical considerations become subordinate to practical ones, since deciding on the theoretical proceedings required for the task at hand is a step that itself calls for the resources that practical reasoning can afford for deciding what is to be done.[19]

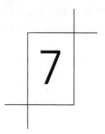

7

Default Reasoning

Default Inference

The topic of default reasoning affords some instructive insights into the nature of the relationship between theoretical and practical reasoning. In logic, a *default* is a fall-back position when drawing a conclusion—a point to which we can appropriately withdraw when things go wrong. But things ought not go wrong in logic. So what is going on here?

Orthodox inferential reasoning proceeds via *logically valid* inference processes that, as such, do—and must—proceed from true premisses to true conclusions. By contrast, default reasoning—which involves an information gap between premisses and conclusions—is such that plausible (though sometimes false) premisses will lead to plausible (though possibly false) conclusions.

The logical validity of inference rules in standard (truth-functional) logic is determined on an input-output basis, a valid rule being one that will invariably yield true outputs (conclusions) from true premisses. All such inference rules will faithfully and unfailingly transmit the truth of premisses to the conclusions. By contrast, the inference processes of default logic are such that the truth of the premisses does not assure the truth of the conclusion but will at most establish that the conclusion is plausible. Such inferences are *ampliative:* the conclusion can go beyond what the premisses guarantee. And this means that such reasonings are fallible and can, and occasionally will, lead from true premisses to false conclusions.

We shall represent *logically valid deducibility* (in its classical construction) by ⊦, and by contrast use ⊪ to represent the *plausible inferability* at issue with default reasoning.

Some examples of inference processes in default logic are as follows:

1. *p* is highly likely ⊪ *p*.
2. *p* is very likely, *q* is very likely ⊪ *p* & *q* is very likely.
3. There is strong evidence in favor of *p* and no more than weak evidence against it ⊪ *p*.
4. *p* has obtained in all past instances ⊪ *p* will obtain in the next instance.

If all we are told of some number is that it is a prime, we would, plausibly enough, conclude that it is not an even integer—even though among an infinity of cases this conclusion could happen to be false. The fact of it is that primes are normally not divisible by 2—that one single case of 2 itself excepted.

As these examples indicate, the inference processes of default logic can all be assimilated to a deductive pattern of the following structure (which does clearly obtain as valid in traditional logic):

- IN ALL ORDINARY (NORMAL, STANDARD, COMMONPLACE) CASES, WHENEVER *P,* THEN *Q*.
- *P* OBTAINS IN THE CASE PRESENTLY AT HAND.
- <THE PRESENT CASE IS AN ORDINARY (NORMAL, STANDARD) ONE.>

∴ *Q* OBTAINS IN THE PRESENT CASE.

Here, that third, usually tacit and thereby enthymematic, premiss plays a pivotal role. And it is, in general, able to do so not because we have secured it as a certified truth, but simply because it is a plausible (albeit defeasible) presumption strongly supported by the available evidence though not, of course, guaranteed. Default reasoning accordingly rests on arguments that would be valid if all of their premisses—explicit and tacit alike—were authentic truths, which they are not since at least one of the critical premises of the argument is no more than a mere presumption.

Such a *defeasible presumption* is emphatically not to be regarded as an established truth but merely something that holds only provisionally, as long as no counterindicatively conflicting information comes to light. Against this background the following procedure is definitively characteristic of default reasoning:

> To treat what is generally (normally, standardly, generally, usually) the case *as if* it were the case always and everywhere and, therefore, as applicable in the present instance

Here, in effect, ignorance is bliss: where there is no good reason to see the case at hand as being out of the ordinary, we simply presume it to be an ordinary one in the absence of visible counterindications. Such reliance on a *principle of presumption* to the effect that what generally holds also holds in the case presently at hand characterizes the modus operandi of default reasoning.[1]

Facing the Prospect of Error

Such plausible presumption can go awry, of course. For it may well happen that the situation at hand fails to be standard and representative of the enthymematic comportment that the argument requires. This is brought out vividly in John Godfry Saxe's poem "The Blind Men and the Elephant," which tells the story of certain blind sages, those "six men of Indostan/To learning much inclined/Who went to see the elephant/(Though all of them were blind)." One sage touched the elephant's "broad and sturdy side" and declared the beast to be "very like a wall." The second, who had felt its tusk, announced the elephant to resemble a spear. The third, who took the elephant's squirming trunk in his hands, compared it to a snake; while the fourth, who put his arm around the elephant's knee, was sure that the animal resembled a tree. A flapping ear convinced another that the elephant had the form of a fan; while the sixth blind man thought that it had the form of a rope, since he had taken hold of the tail.

> *And so these men of Indostan,*
> *Disputed loud and long;*
> *Each in his own opinion*
> *Exceeding stiff and strong:*
> *Though each was partly in the right,*
> *And all were in the wrong.*

None of those blind sages was altogether in error; it is just that the facts at their disposal were nontypical and unrepresentative in a way that gave them a biased and misleading picture of reality. It is not that they did not know truth, but rather that an altogether plausible inference from the truth they knew propelled them into error.

Since such a policy of typicality presumption may well lead us down the primrose path into error, how is it ever to be justified? The answer here lies precisely in the consideration that what is at issue is not a truth claim but a policy of procedure. And such policies of procedure are not justified in the theoretical (that is, factual) order but in the practical or pragmatic order of deliberation. The validation at issue runs roughly as follows:

1. We have questions to which we need a (satisfactory) answer, and in the face of this we take the stance that . . .
2. We are rationally entitled to use a premiss that holds good promise of finding one (that is, is effective or more effective than the other available alternatives) even though it may occasionally fail.

On this basis we proceed subject to the idea that if and when things go wrong, this is a bridge we can cross when we get there, invoking "explanations" and excuses to indicate the unusual (anormal, extraordinary) circumstances of the case. Even as in real life we cannot manage our affairs sensibly without running risks, so in the cognitive life we must, on occasion, take in stride the risk of error, since the inevitable result of a radical risk-nothing policy is the have-nothing stance of radical skepticism. And this situation is particularly prominent in inductive contexts.

Induction as Default Reasoning

The term *induction* is derived from the Latin rendering of Aristotle's *epagôgê*—the process for moving to a generalization from its specific instances.[2] Gradually extended over an increasingly wide range, induction can be seen as a question-answering device encompassing virtually the whole range of nondeductive reasoning. Thus, consider a typical inductive argument: from "All the magnets we have examined attract iron filings" we arrive at "All magnets attract iron filings." It would be deeply problematic to regard this as a deductive argument that rests on the (obviously false) premiss: "What is the case in all examined instances is universally the case." Rather, what we have here is a plausible presumption that takes the cases in hand to be typical and generally representative in the absence of concrete counterindications—that is, we have an instance of default reasoning.

Induction, so regarded, is accordingly not so much a process of *inference* as one of presumption-based *truth-estimation*. We clearly want to accomplish our explanatory gap-filling in the least risky, minimally problematic way, as determined by plausibilistic considerations. This is illustrated by such examples as:

- THERE IS SMOKE YONDER.
- USUALLY, WHERE(EVER) THERE'S SMOKE, THERE'S FIRE.
- <THE PRESENT SITUATION FITS THE USUAL RUN.>

∴ THERE IS FIRE YONDER.

or, again,

- Two-thirds of the items in the sample are defective.
- <The sample is representative of the whole.>

∴ Two-thirds of the items in the whole population are defective.

(Here the enthymematically tacit premisses needed to make the argument deductively cogent have been indicated.)

Its reliance on a presumption of typicality, normalcy, or the like means that any inductive process is inherently chancy. Induction rests on presumption-geared default reasoning, and its conclusions are thus always at risk to further or better data, since what looks to be typical or representative may in due course turn out not to be so.

Default Reasoning as Nonmonotonic

Since default reasonings rest on a presumption of normality, typicality, or the like, it may well transpire that while a premiss $\Vdash$ implies a certain conclusion, the conjunction of this premiss with some further propositions may, nevertheless, fail to do so. Such implications are called nonmonotonic because, while "If p then q" obtains, it, nevertheless, can happen that q sometimes fails to obtain in certain circumstances, where p holds, so that

$$p \Rightarrow q \text{ need not yield } (p \ \& \ r) \Rightarrow q.$$

Additional information can destabilize default implications.

Clearly, the reason why the monotonicity-characterizing principle
Whenever $p \vdash q$, then $(p \ \& \ r) \vdash q$

works in deductive context is that here there is then no normality linkage between p and q that requires the addition of further material that may or may not be forthcoming—in accordance with a stipulation of normalcy or of "all things being equal" in the case of inductive reasonings. The reliance of default reasoning on a presumption of normality, typicality, or the like, means that throughout this domain new information can undo earlier findings.

Thus, consider the following claim:
> If you are in America, then you might be in New York.

This is, of course, perfectly correct. But it will not do to "strengthen" the antecedent:
> If you are in America and you are in Texas, then you might be in New York.

The conclusions we arrive at with nonmonotonic implication relationships are no more than presumptions. For in making the inference we have to presume that the situation is not one where some yet unseen conclusion-averting circumstance comes into play.

This state of affairs also means that with nonmonotonic implications *modus ponens* fails: the combination of p and $p \Rightarrow q$ need not *demonstrate* that q obtains but may do no more than to establish a *presumption* to that effect.[3] Nonmonotonicity is thus a standard feature of default inference as is illustrated by contrasting this:
> If I had put sugar in the tea, then it would have tasted fine.

with this:
> If I had put sugar and cayenne pepper in the tea, then it would have tasted fine.

Or, again, contrast:
> If you greet him, he will answer politely.

with
> If you greet him with an insult, he will answer politely.

After all, that first implication effectively (but tacitly) comes to this:
> If you greet him *in the usual and ordinary way,* he will answer politely.

And the antecedent of the second implication violates that initial condition.

With default inferences we have to deal with what is, from the standpoint of standard logic, a decidedly eccentric mode of reasoning. For no qualification additional to the antecedent as such can abrogate what a valid monotonic implication implies: the antecedent will, in and of itself, suffice to guarantee the consequent. But whenever that "inevitably (invariably, unavoidably)" becomes weakened to "generally, usually, probably, possibly)," the monotonicity that is requisite for authentic implication is lost. To obtain a conclusion we must now suppose that nothing untoward is hidden from our sight—that nothing unmentioned intervenes. And this always brings the factor of presumption upon the scene.

Some Comforting Considerations

What if those normality presumptions should prove unjustified? How are we to proceed in the context of conclusions arrived at by reasoning that we see as potentially misleading? The short answer is, Cautiously! But a somewhat more informative response lies in the important prospect of *blurring* that conclusion—making it less specified and detailed. As stated at the outset default reasoning calls for the possibility of resort to a fall-back position. And in managing our cognitive risks we can always fall back upon *vagueness* and its inherent qualifications.

With default reasoning in general and induction in particular we run the risk that our conclusions may run awry thanks to our reliance on (generally tacit) suppositions of normality or typicality that may fail in the circumstances at hand. To offset the risk error we can resort to the introduction of decreasing definiteness for the sake of increasing security. Thus, instead of reasoning the following:

- q IS HIGHLY LIKELY WHEREVER p.
- IN THE PRESENT CASE p OBTAINS.
- THE PRESENT CASE LOOKS TO BE A TYPICAL, MAJORITY-CONFORMING ONE.
- <LOOKS ARE NOT DECEIVING HERE.>

∴ IN THE PRESENT CASE q OBTAINS

We would instead reason to
   In the present case *q* probably obtains,

thereby taking a sensible step in the direction of safety. But, of course, likelihoods do not answer yes/no questions, and where such questions confront us, we have little choice but to resort (circumstances permitting) to chance the risks of the presumption of typicality/normality that characterizes default reasoning. There are, however, some promising precautions here. After all, a fundamental feature of inquiry is represented by the following observation:

> Thesis 1: *Insofar as our thinking is vague, truth is accessible even in the face of error.*

Consider the situation where you correctly accept *P*-or-*Q*. But— so let it be supposed—the truth of this disjunction roots entirely in *P*, whereas *Q* is quite false. However, you accept *P*-or-*Q* only because you are convinced of the truth of *Q*; it so happens that *P* is something you actually disbelieve. Yet, despite your error, your belief is entirely true.[4] Consider a concrete instance. You believe that Mr. Kim Ho is Korean because you believe him to be a North Korean. However, he is a South Korean, something you would flatly reject. Nevertheless, your belief that he is Korean is unquestionably correct. Thanks to the indefiniteness of that disjunctive belief at issue, the error in which you are involved, although real, is not so grave as to destabilize the truth of your belief. This example illustrates a more far-reaching point:

> Thesis 2: *There is, in general, an inverse relationship between the precision or definiteness of a judgment and its security: detail and probability stand in a competing relationship.*

It is a basic principle of epistemology that increased confidence in the correctness of our estimates can always be purchased at the price of decreased accuracy. We *estimate* the height of the tree at around twenty-five feet. We are *quite sure* that the tree is twenty-five feet plus or minus five feet. We are *virtually certain* that its height is twenty-five feet plus or minus ten feet. But we are *completely and absolutely sure* that its height is between one inch and one hundred yards. Of this we are completely sure, in the sense that we deem it absolutely certain, secure beyond the shadow of a doubt, as certain as we can be of anything in the world, so sure that we would be willing to stake our life on it, and the like. With any sort of estimate, there is always a characteristic trade-off between the evidential *security* of the estimate (as determinable on the basis of its probability or degree of acceptability) and the informative *definiteness* (exactness, detail, precision) of its asserted content. Vaguer and looser statements are for that very reason more secure because they embody larger margins of error. This relationship between security and definiteness is graphically characterized by a curve of the general form of an equilateral hyperbola (see display 5), and this sort of relationship holds just as well for our *truth* estimates as of others.

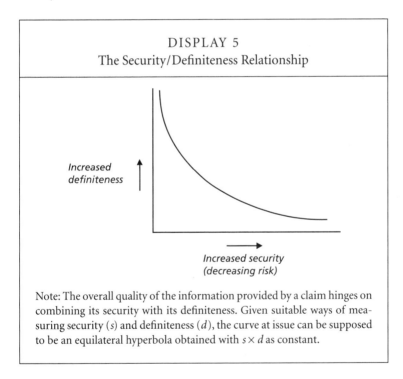

DISPLAY 5
The Security/Definiteness Relationship

Increased definiteness

Increased security (decreasing risk)

Note: The overall quality of the information provided by a claim hinges on combining its security with its definiteness. Given suitable ways of measuring security (s) and definiteness (d), the curve at issue can be supposed to be an equilateral hyperbola obtained with $s \times d$ as constant.

This state of affairs has far-reaching consequences. In particular, it means that no secure statement about objective reality can say exactly and in complete detail how matters stand universally always and everywhere. To capture the truth of things by means of language we must proceed by way of "warranted approximation." In general we can be sure of how things "usually" are and how they "roughly" are, but not how they always and exactly are. And this impels our reasoning in the direction of presuppositions of normalcy, typicality, and the like, which are characteristic of default argumentation.

Be this as it may, however, the present considerations indicate that inductive inference as traditionally conceived affords a paradigm instance of default reasoning, which itself emerges in their light as an exercise in standard deductive inference subject to a recourse to the potentially defeasible presumption of typicality.

Yet how is the adoption of a potentially defeasible thesis to qualify as rationally appropriate? The answer, as noted above, lies in the general principle of risk management. For what is at issue with presumption is at bottom not an endorsement of a truth but adoption of a policy. And rationality here—as elsewhere in matters of practical procedure—pivots on the principle of a favorable balance of potential benefit over potential loss. In many situations default reasoning affords our best-available pathway to our ultimately very practical need for information—for answering in a cogent and epistemically responsible way a question that we need to resolve.

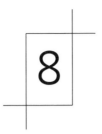

Cognitive Myopia and the World's Lawfulness

The Idea of Cognitive Myopia

Our species is *Homo sapiens:* "man the knower." Neither instinct nor necessity is the determinative factor shaping our actions in this world, but each influences the choices we make on the basis of the information we are able to secure. For us, knowledge is at once theoretically satisfying and practically indispensable. And this teleology of knowledge—the range of purpose that it serves for us—exerts a powerful formative influence on both the manner and the means of our securing, organizing, and applying the information we are able to obtain regarding the world and our situation within it. After all, knowledge is itself a powerfully practical tool for creatures constituted as we are, whose actions in the world are determined not by automatic reflexes or by Pavlovian conditioning, but by our beliefs.

Against this background, the guiding idea of this chapter's deliberations lies in the following two considerations:

1. Our only cognitive access to reality (R) comes via a model (M) that we make of reality to serve as its artifactually thought-contrived surrogate.
2. Theoretical reflection and historical experience alike conjoin to indicate that we have good reason to think that even our best

model (M) of reality (R) is in some respects discrepant from it—that we have not and will never be able to manage to get it all just right.

In this context, it is instructive to exploit a fundamental analogy of conception to perception, seeing that it makes sense to conceive of the relationship of M to R on analogy of sight, with R akin to the actual scene that one confronts and M akin to one's visualization of it. This means that even as sight can be and often is myopic in blurring details so as to preclude the discernment of real differences, so exactly the same sort of thing can happen with our conception of things. Here, too, one can fail to recognize real differences. And just as with *visual* phenomena, the *conceptual* phenomena we confront in the process of theorizing can, and generally do, fail to do full justice to a reality whose complex detail calls for more sophisticated descriptions and characterization than we currently have at our disposal.

Accordingly, one can envision both as to perception and as to conception the operation of a difference-obscuring myopia that admits of two related modes of item assimilation:

- *Confusing* one item with a somewhat similar item from which it is actually different
- *Conflating* two actually different items by failing to notice their differences

With *perception* the "items" at issue are, of course, different physical states, objects of some sort, whereas with *conception* the items are different fact-characterizing propositions. What concerns us here is the *process of representation,* which involves taking one item (the "object," the "reality") and letting another (the "model," the "appearance") represent it. In such a representational process the "model" or "appearance" *is taken to stand as* a surrogate for the "reality" being represented. This sort of modeling or representation occurs in particular in the setting of two sorts of reality/appearance contrasts:

Reality (R)	Appearance/ Model (M)
Physical states of affairs	Symbolic descriptions
Actual facts	Putative facts

What will thus concern us here is the nature of the relationships between reality (R) and perceived appearance (A) on the perceptual side, and between reality (R) and its explanatory model (M) on the conceptual side.

The first consequence of taking a myopia-contemplating perspective is that one had best show some respect for the Kantian distinction between reality itself and the empirical reality represented by our best-made conceptualization of it. For the latter can at best be deemed to be an estimate (and at most a nebulous approximation) of the former. This consideration means that in respect to the relationship of M to R, our deliberations can only proceed along the *via negativa*. We can make a good many plausible contentions about what does *not* hold for R (for example, we are not in a position to claim that it is identical to M), but we cannot say anything directly and positively about it. For, of course, we have no way of characterizing reality *apart* from our would-be conceptualizations of it. The only reality to which we have cognitive access is that depicted in our models of the real. We know nothing in detail about reality's imperfections, although we cannot avoid acknowledging that they exist.

This inability to be descriptively positive about R by way of comparison or contrast with M does not mean that we cannot proceed here in the language of hypothesis, of assumption and supposition. And this is exactly what the present discussion proposes to do. We all, for the most part, recognize that our knowledge of the world's ways is in various respects incomplete and imperfect. But the implications of this fairly unavoidable acknowledgement have not been sufficiently noted. For insofar as a cognitive gap exists between reality itself and our appearance-based apprehension of it, there is going to be a lack of coordination—of consonance and agreement—between the two so that just this cannot also be said regarding our model (M) of reality (R). This will manifest itself at various levels, particularly in the following two:

- *Natural occurrence versus cognitive apprehension* as reflected in the contrast between the order of physical process and its mental characterization in the perceptual order of the appearances as we apprehend them via propositionalized thought

- *Physical reality versus modeling thereof* as reflected in the contrast between the existential order of things and their representation in the cognitive representations afforded by our scientific models

At both of these levels we cannot but suppose that the sort of imperfect representation that may be characterized as *cognitive myopia* is rooted in *the inability to distinguish differences.* (To be sure, we here construe this phenomenon in a broader than ordinary way, because as its broad-stroke characterization as *cognitive* myopia indicates, it will be taken to relate not only to matters of imperfect *perception* but to matters of imperfect *conception* as well.)

How Cognitive Myopia Functions

In the wake of an ever more sophisticated technology for acquiring and processing data, the progress of science is such that increasingly sophisticated distinctions have to be drawn and increasingly refined theories employed to discriminate that which an earlier and cruder state of the art failed to take into account.[1] This situation typifies what we characterize here as cognitive myopia.

Specifically, the key ideas at issue here are to be understood as follows:
- *X confuses* items x and y over the question-manifold Q iff in answering the questions within this manifold X fails to distinguish between x and y.
- *X conflates* items x and y over the question-manifold Q iff *in answering the question within the manifold, X sees both x and y as one selfsame z.*

As noted above, this cognitive myopia takes two forms:
- *Mild version:* This involves an *occasional confusion* between two distinct sorts of items (such as when there is an occasional mix-up in construing h as k, or conversely).
- *Strong version:* This involves a *systemic conflation* (such as when both h and k appear simply as a fuzzy and indistinguishable blurred complex).

For the sake of illustration consider someone whose visual myopia is such that he is incompetent with regard to telling 5 and 6 apart. As a result of such an inability to distinguish 5 from 6 the individual may well, through *conflation*,

envision 56 as **✷✷**.

Or, again, the individual may, through *confusion*,

envision 56 as 66.

Such forms of cognitive myopia have very different ramifications for our grasp of the world's lawful comportment.

Consequences of Cognitive Myopia

Suppose that we are in reality dealing with the perfectly regular series

R: 6 5 6 5 6 5 6 5 6 5 . . .

But due to the occasional confusion of a mild cognitive myopia we may then actually "see" this series (be it by way of observation or conceptualization) as

M: 6 5 5 5 6 5 5 5 6 5 . . .

Observe that our inability to distinguish has in this case effectively transmuted a lawful regularity into a random disorder. It is then clear (via "Mill's methods of agreement and difference") that there is no causal correlation between *R* and *M*. The supposition of (mild) myopia thus induces a drastic disconnection between the two levels of consideration at issue, with the lawful order of *R* giving way to lawlessness in regard to its model *M*.

Thus, even so crude an example suffices to show that lawful order can unravel and be destroyed by the confusion engendered by an occasional inability to discern differences. This relatively rudimentary observation has far-reaching implications. Specifically, it means that even if the world is possessed of a highly lawful order, this feature of reality may well fail to be captured in even a mildly myopic representation of it. This, in turn, means that, given myopia, the worldview presented in our world-modeling may well be no more than loosely coupled to the underlying reality of things.

Observe that, as a consequence of this situation, even an elegant physical order (ϕ) may well be reflected confusedly at the cognitive/psychological level (ψ) in such a way that its representation there involves a substantially random and disordered phenomenology. Thus, a lawful determinism of physical order may well be decoupled from the more randomized indeterminism that prevails at the cognitive/psychological level in the realm of thought.

Given that rational agents act within nature on the basis of their understanding of things, it will transpire that even in an otherwise lawful and deterministic world this order will break down once imperfectly intelligent agents evolve and cognitive myopia deconstructs the world's lawful order. Thus, let it be specific that such an agent acts according to the *rule of behavior* (be it internally or externally mandated):

Wherever you see a 5, do *A* but otherwise do not.

Then in our prior hypothetical example of 5-6 confusion the agent will produce the following behavior sequence:

$A - - A\,A\,A - A - - - \ldots$

The agent has thus inserted into physical reality what is (via our hypotheses) an essentially random sequence. Our hypotheses of mildly myopic perception has transmuted that supposedly lawful and deterministic world into one that is (in at least one respect) lawless and random—even at the level of its physical comportment. Myopic perception at the level of appearance (*A*) has introduced a randomness-productive disconnection between the level of actual physical phenomenology (*R*) and that of beckoned operations (*B*).

Ramifications of Conflation

There is also the prospect of a severe cognitive myopia that results in a *systemic conflation* of reality in the setting of its conceptualization.

For the sake of illustration, let it be the case that the reality that confronts us has the random structure

6 5 5 6 6 6 5 5 5 6 5 5 6 6 5 ...

But let it also be that in representing this reality in our observations and/or conceptualization our vision of the matter is so myopic that we cannot readily distinguish between 5 and 6: both simply look like a blurring (5-or-6) to us. Then the above chaotic series is representatively transmuted into the elegant uniformity of the series

(5-or-6)(5-or-6)(5-or-6)(5-or-6) ...

Where reality is in fact random and discordant, its representation in our cognitive field of vision is the quintessence of lawful elegance.

This brings a portentous prospect in its wake. For it means that a world that is substantially lawless in some respect or other at the level of its physical operations may well appear in the eyes of a sufficiently myopic observer to be the very height of lawfulness. Here, too, the loose coupling between reality and our representation of it can create a substantial discrepancy. But this now arises in the reverse manner from that contemplated above. For under the conditions at issue we have it that

1. A world whose physical comportment is in certain respect random and lawless may well be seen by its cognitively imperfect observers as having a phenomenology that is deterministically lawful.

2. There is the prospect that a cognitive psychological phenomenology that is deterministically lawful may exist in—and thus be grossly misunderstood—a physical order that is substantially chaotic and random.

It is possible in this way to introduce a deterministic regularity of operation at the psychological and thereby behavioral level even into an otherwise indeterministic world.

For the sake of illustration, let it be that very different physical configurations or processes can yield one selfsame psychic result in different ways, even as a balance scale can be tilted to the left or right either by adding weights to one side or by removing them from the other. A person who then merely observes how the scale is tilted cannot tell what happened to produce this result and cannot discriminate between the more-on-the-left and the less-on-the right situation.

In this way, even an ontology in which beliefs are wholly the product of physiological brain states may nevertheless be unable to discriminate between different physiological states that produce the same belief result. So even physically determined beliefs may well leave the psychical situation underdetermined. That is, even a world characterized by a strictly deterministic physical system may leave the psychic situation in a state of myopic confusion or conflation.

Problems of Lawfulness

The preceding deliberations have contemplated two forms of cognitive myopia that differ significantly in their implications. But both conspire to raise the prospect of a significant decoupling between the order of reality (R) and our cognitive apprehension of it (A), between the lawful order of nature (N) and its representation in thought (T), between the realities of physics (ϕ) and the phenomenology of psychologically mediated conceptualization (ψ). This circumstance yields the prospect that the order of nature *as we apprehend it* is not unequivocally determined by the existential order of nature in and of itself but will be an artifact of our cognitive resources for its conceptualization. For reality as we human inquirers have it is not something that lies one-sidedly with reality itself but also—and significantly— with our mode of apprehending it. In particular, the character of our apprehended world as orderly, lawful, and deterministic depends not just on the world itself but also on the extent to which cognitive myopia afflicts the representational fruits of our investigation. In a significant way, the world's discernible lawfulness is destined to lie in the workings of the beholder's eyes.

This situation has further significant consequences. A world is equipped with intelligent agents insofar as it contains cognition-capable creatures that shape their deliberate actions with reference to their thought models of the world. The actions of such beings are determined via their ideas and opinions about what goes on: it is the *putative* condition of things that impels such beings into action—irrespective of what the *actual* condition of things may be. Evolutionary pressures only go so far in enforcing a coordination here. Consequently, insofar as there can be a disconnection between the lawful nature of the world and the modus operandi of its intelligent agents, there arises the prospect that the thoughts and actions of these beings will be out of step with the lawfulness (or lawlessness, as the case may be) of the remaining sectors of natural reality.

Accordingly, the lesson of these deliberations is that the nomic regularity we discern in the world—its lawful order—will be as much a feature of the investigative intelligence at work as of the modus operandi of the world's processes themselves. Myopia can make all the difference here. Confusion can create disorder where there is order; conflation can make order out of disorder. We have to face the prospect that, to a substantial extent, the world's lawful order as best we can determine it may lie in the eyes of the beholder. An intelligent being who is subject to cognitive myopia is really not in a position to decide with assured confidence whether the reality that it inhabits is ultimately lawful or lawless and random. We cognitively imperfect, myopic intelligences cannot hope to achieve a definitive finding on the fundamental metaphysical issue of determinism versus indeterminism (randomness). For us finite and imperfect inquirers, the key question of the world's constitution in this regard is decisively undecidable.

Nihilism and Skepticism Find No Support in Cognitive Myopia

Does not the prospect of such a disconnection between appearance and reality lead straightaway to drastic skepticism? Not necessarily! For, as we saw in the preceding chapter, one fundamental feature of inquiry is represented by the following consideration:

> *By constraining us to make vaguer judgments, the ignorance reflected in cognitive myopia enhances our access to correct information (albeit at the cost of less detail and precision).*

Thus, if I have forgotten that Seattle is in Washington State, then if "forced to guess" I might well erroneously locate it in Oregon. Nevertheless, my vague judgment that "Seattle is located in the northwestern United States" is quite correct. This state of affairs means that when the truth of our claims is critical we generally "play it safe" and make our commitments less definite and detailed. Vagueness effectively provides a protective shell to guard that statement against a charge of falsity. Irrespective of how matters might actually stand within a vast range of alternative circumstances and conditions, the statement remains secure, its truth unaffected by which possibility is realized. In sum, cognitive myopia does not constrain skepticism by blocking the way to the realization of truth when we cease to operate at the level of precise detail. For it is not the truth but the detailed truth that is bound to be inaccessible to beings afflicted by cognitive myopia. And—most fundamentally—its *failings* in point of completeness and definitiveness detract neither from the theoretical value that can be ascribed to our imperfect information about the world nor from the practical utility that this knowledge has for us.[2]

Notes

CHAPTER 1: PERSONAL EXPERIENCE AND REALISTIC ONTOLOGY

1. To be sure, abstract things, such as colors or numbers, will not have dispositional properties. For being divisible by four is not a disposition of sixteen. Plato got the matter right in Book VII of the *Republic:* in the realm of abstracta, such as those of mathematics, there are not genuine processes—and process is a requisite of dispositions. Of course, there may be dispositional truths in which numbers (or colors) figure—for example, relating to my predilection for odd numbers. But if a truth (or supposed truth) does no more than to convey how someone thinks about a thing, then it does not indicate any property of the thing itself.

2. This aspect of objectivity was justly stressed in the "Second Analogy" of Kant's *Critique of Pure Reason,* though his discussion rests on ideas already contemplated by Leibniz, *Philosophische Schriften,* ed. C. I. Gerhardt (Berlin: Weidmann, 1860–1890), 7:319ff.

3. See C. I. Lewis, *An Analysis of Knowledge and Valuation* (La Salle, IL: Open Court, 1962), 180–81.

4. On related issues, see also the author's *Realistic Pragmatism* (Albany, NY: State University of New York Press, 2000).

CHAPTER 2: REALISM IN PRAGMATIC PERSPECTIVE

1. Immanuel Kant held that we cannot experientially learn though perception about the objective reality of outer things, because we can only recognize our perceptions as *perceptions* (that is, representations of outer things) if these outer things are supposed as such from the first (rather than being learned or inferred from representations). As he summarizes the matter in the "Refutation of Idealism": "Idealism assumed that the only immediate experience is inner experience, and that from it we can only *infer* outer things—and this, moreover, only in an untrustworthy manner. . . . But in the above proof it has been shown that outer experience is really immediate" (*CPuR,* B276). Here "is really immediate" is to be construed as: "must be accepted noninferentially from the very outset, because inference could not accomplish what is needed to arrive at those outer things."

2. Maimonides, *The Guide for the Perplexed,* trans. M. Friedländer (London: George Routledge & Sons, 1904), I:71, 96a.

3. The justification of such imputations is treated more fully in chap. 9 of the author's *Induction* (Oxford: Blackwell, 1980).

4. Charles S. Peirce, *Collected Papers,* ed. C. Hartshorne and P. Weiss (Cambridge MA: Harvard University Press, 1934), vol. 5, sect. 5.383.

5. Compare the discussion of cognate issues in the author's *Methodological Pragmatism* (Oxford: Basil Blackwell, 1977).

6. In English, we have no one-word verb "to make possible" akin to the German *ermoeglichen,* apart from the obsolete *possibilitate,* nowadays known only to readers of the *Oxford English Dictionary.* To adopt "possibilize" for this purpose would perhaps be sensible and certainly convenient.

7. The author's *Empirical Inquiry* (Totowa, NJ: Rowman & Littlefield, 1982) and his *Realistic Pragmatism* (Albany, NY: SUNY Press, 2000) are relevant to some of this chapter's themes.

CHAPTER 3: PRESUPPOSITIONAL REALISM AND JUSTIFACTORY IDEALISM

1. This also explains why the dispute over mathematical realism (Platonism) has little bearing on the issue of physical realism. Mathematical entities are akin to fictional entities in this—that we can only say about them what we can extract by deductive means from what we have explicitly put into their defining characterization. These abstract entities do not have nongeneric properties, since each is a "lowest species" unto itself.

2. The point is Kantian in its orientation. Kant holds that we cannot experientially learn through our perceptions about the objectivity of outer things, because we can only recognize our perceptions as perceptions (that is, representations of outer things) if these outer things are given as such from the first (rather than being learned or inferred).

3. Thus, spots in the visual field, identifiable to no one save the subject, qualify as identifiable items. The identificatory transaction is multipersonal in the *standard* cases, but not always; paradigmatically and generally, but not inevitably.

4. Issues relevant to this chapter's deliberations are also discussed in the author's "An Idealistic Realism" in *The Blackwell Guide to Metaphysics,* ed. Richard Gale (Oxford: Blackwell, 2002): 242–62.

CHAPTER 4: RATIONAL ECONOMY AND THE EVOLUTIONARY IMPETUS

1. St. Thomas Aquinas, *Summa Theologica,* Q. 79, art. 11.

2. Historically, the doctrine of the primacy of practical over theoretical reason goes back to Schopenhauer's teaching that the intellect is altogether the servant of the will. The Schopenhaurian thesis that cognition is subordinate to the will is elaborated by R. H. Lotze and Christoph Sigwart; see the Introduction to part 2 of his *Logic,* trans. H. Dendy (London, 1895; orig. German edition, Leipzig, 1878). From these writers the theory moves on the German side to neo-Kantian

thinkers—such as Hans Vaihinger—who stress the prominence of practical reason, and on the American side through Peirce and James to the later pragmatists. (Note that James explicitly quotes Sigwart with approval.)

3. C. S. Peirce, *Collected Papers* (Cambridge, MA: Harvard University Press 1934), vol. 5, sect. 5.366.

CHAPTER 5: SPECIFICITY PRIORITIZATION AND
THE PRIMACY OF THE PARTICULAR

1. To be sure, as Pierre Duhem insisted, a theory-observation clash will in general involve a plurality of participating theories, so that it will not be clear which particular theory will have to be jettisoned. See his *The Aim and Structure of Physical Theory,* trans. P. Wiener (Princeton, NJ: Princeton University Press, 1982).

2. *Essays on the Intellectual Powers of Man,* vol. 6 (Edinburgh: John Bell, 1785), 4:570.

3. *An Inquiry into the Human Mind,* vol. 1 (1764), v (Hamilton edition, p. 102b).

4. See Arthur Fine, "The Natural Ontological Attitude," in *Scientific Realism,* ed. Jarret Lephon (Berkeley: University of California Press, 1984), 83–107, esp. p. 85. The maxim is articulated in line with David Hilbert's endeavor to demonstrate the consistency of set theory on a more concrete non-set-theoretical basis.

5. On counterfactual conditionals and their problems, see the author's *Hypothetical Reasoning* (Amsterdam: North Holland, 1964); David Lewis, *Conditionals* (Oxford: Blackwell, 1973); Ernest Sosa, ed., *Causation and Conditionals* (London: Oxford University Press, 1975); Anthony Appiah, *Assertion and Conditionals* (Cambridge: Cambridge University Press, 1985); and Frank Johnson, ed., *Conditionals* (Oxford: Clarendon Press, 1991).

6. In this context, however, it is important that the generalization at issue be seen as somehow lawful and not as merely a fortuitous and accidental aggregation of special cases, so that the factor of generality is present in name only.

7. This issue is addressed in E. W. Adams "Subjective and Indicative Conditionals," *Foundations of Language* (1970), 6:39–94.

8. See the author's "Belief-Contravening Suppositions," *The Philosophical Review* 70 (1961): 176–96; and *Hypothetical Reasoning* (Amsterdam: North Holland, 1964).

CHAPTER 6: DISMISSING EXTREMELY REMOTE POSSIBILITIES

1. Recent probability theorists concerned with inductive issues have dealt with infinitesimal probabilities almost exclusively in the context of the probability of scientific generalizations and laws. See Richard C. Jeffrey, *The Logic of Decision,* 2nd ed. (Chicago, IL: University of Chicago Press, 1983), 190–95; and John Earman, *Bayes or Bust* (Cambridge, MA: MIT Press, 1992), 86–95). The epistemic acceptability of propositions is, of course, something rather different from the action-guiding concerns of decision theory.

2. "Les probabilities qui s'expriment par un number inférieur à 10^{-1000} son non seulenent négligeables dams la pratique conrante de la vie, mais unversalle-ment negligeables . . . ; pour le savant elles *sont* nulls et les phenomènes auxquels elles se supportest sont absolumnet impossibles." Emile Borel, *Valeur pratique et philosophie des probabilities* (Paris: Gauthier-Villars, 1939), 156. The entire section "fur les probabilities invesellement négligibles" (pp. 154–56) is saliently relevant to the present topic.

3. Paul Slovic et al., "Preference for Insuring Against Probable Small Losses: Insurance Implications," *Journal of Risk and Insurance* 44 (1977), 254.

4. David Lewis, "Causal Decision Theory," *Australasian Journal of Philosophy* 59 (1981), 14.

5. Various writers speak here of *practical* certainty, *Certitude pratique*. (Cf. Borel, *Valeur pratique*, 28.

6. U.S. Food and Drug Administration, "Chemical Compounds in Food-pro-cessing Animals: Criteria and Procedures for Evaluating Assays of Carcinogenic Residues," *Federal Register* 44 (March 20, 1979): 17070–17114.

7. U.S. Atomic Energy Commission [U.S. Nuclear Regulatory Commission], *An Assessment of Accident Risks in U.S. Commercial Nuclear Power Plants* (Wash-ington, D.C., 1974); summary volume, AEC Publication WASH-1400 (August 1974). Quoted in William W. Lowrance, *Of Acceptable Risk: Science and the De-termination of Safety* (Los Altos, CA: Kaufmann, 1976), 73.

8. R. W. Kates, "Hazard and Choice Perception in Flood Plain Management," Research Paper no. 78 (Chicago, IL: Department of Geography, University of Chicago, 1962).

9. J. P. Holdren, "The Nuclear Controversy and the Limitations of Decision Making by Experts," *Bulletin of the Atomic Scientists* 32 (1976): 20–22.

10. G. W. Fairley, "Criteria for Evaluating the 'Small' Probability of a Cata-strophic Accident from the Marine Transportation of Liquefied Natural Gas," in *Risk-benefit Methodology and Application: Some Papers Presented at the Engineering Foundation Workshop, Asilomar,* ed. D. Okrent, UCLA-ENG 7598 (Los Angeles: University of California, Department of Energy and Kinetics, 1975); Baruch Fischoff, "Cost-benefit Analysis and the Art of Motorcycle Maintenance," *Policy Sci-ences* 8 (1977): 177–202; A. E. Green and A. J. Bourne, *Reliability Technology* (New York: Wiley-Interscience, 1972); Paul Slovic, "Behavioral Decision Theory," *Annu-al Review of Psychology* 28 (1977): 1–39; and A. Tversky and D. Kahneman, "Judg-ment Under Uncertainty: Heuristics and Biases," *Science* 185 (1974): 1124–31.

11. See Kenneth J. Arrow, "Alternative Approaches to the Theory of Choice in Risk-Taking Situations," *Econometrica* 19 (1951): 414.

12. Bernoulli's original 1730 essay "Specimen theoriae novae de mensura sor-tis" is translated into German by A. Pringsheim as *Versuch einer neuen Theorie von Glücksfällen* (Leipzig, 1896). For an instructive discussion see Borel, *Valeur pra-tique,* 60–66.

13. See Richard Jeffrey, *The Logic of Decision*, 2nd ed. (Chicago: University of Chicago Press, 1983): 151–55. The classical approach of Bernoulli himself was to conduct the evaluative process in terms of utility rather than money, envisioning the utility of money to decline exponentially with amount. Another approach is to deploy Herbert Simon's conception of satisfying with its view that "enough is enough." See Michael A. Slote, *Beyond Optimizing* (Cambridge, MA: Harvard University Press, 1989).

14. It is also possible to entertain the idea of utter catastrophes conceived of as "unacceptable" possibilities that one would not be prepared to risk under any circumstances—no matter how small the possibility of their being realized. But this poses different issues and leads into other directions than those presently in view.

15. On the opposite side of the coin lies the distinction between mere disasters and outright catastrophes—the latter being eventuations so horrendous that we would in no circumstances accept any course of action that involves a probability of realization greater than genuine zero. On this issue, see the author's *Risk* (Lanham, MD: University Press of America, 1983), 75–76.

16. On the lottery paradox, see Henry E. Kyburg Jr., *Probability and the Logic of Rational Belief* (Middletown, CT: Wesleyan University Press, 1961); J. L. Cohen, *The Probable and the Provable* (Oxford: Clarendon, 1977); and Robert Stalnaker, *Inquiry* (Cambridge, MA: MIT Press, 1984).

17. The German proverb has it that "Kleinvieh macht auch Mist" (even small animals make dung). More seriously, a wide spectrum of trivially small risks can become collectively nontrivial, which is why people go to Lloyds for insurance.

18. This proviso will require setting the boundaries for what is to be a single decision context. But this issue, while not without its difficulties, involves ultimately manageable complexities that lead beyond the limits of the present deliberations.

19. Some of the issues in this chapter were also discussed in the author's *Risk* (Lanham, MD: University Press of America, 1983), 35–40. I am grateful to Ben Eggleston for constructive comments on a draft of this chapter.

CHAPTER 7: DEFAULT REASONING

1. Regarding default reasoning and its ramifications, see "Common-Sense Reasoning" in *The Routledge Encyclopedia of Philosophy* (London: Routledge, 2000); William L. Harper, "A Sketch of Some Recent Developments in the Theory of Conditionals," in *IFS: Conditionals, Belief, Decision, Chance and Time*, ed. W. L. Harper, L. G. Pearson, and R. Stalnaker (Dordrecht: D. Reidel, 1981); Henry E. Kyburg Jr. and Chon Man Teng, *Uncertain Inference* (Cambridge: Cambridge University Press, 2001); J. L. Pollock, "A Theory of Defeasible Reasoning," *International Journal of Intelligent Systems* 6 (1991): 33–54; R. Reiter, "Nonmonotonic Reasoning," *Annual Review of Cognitive Science* 2 (1987): 147–86; and the author's *Induction* (Oxford: Basil Blackwell, 1980).

2. See W. D. Ross, *Aristotle's Prime and Posterior Analytics* (Oxford: Clarendon Press, 1949), 47–51.

3. On nonmonotonic inference, see J. L. Pollock, "A Theory of Defeasible Reasoning," *International Journal of Intelligent Systems* 6 (1991): 33–54; and R. Reiter, "Nonmonotonic Reasoning," *Annual Review of Cognitive Science* 2 (1987): 147–86.

4. Examples of this sort indicate why philosophers are unwilling to identify *knowledge* with *true belief.*

Chapter 8: Cognitive Myopia and the World's Lawfulness

1. On this topic, see the author's *Scientific Progress* (Oxford: Blackwell, 1978).

2. After all, in practical matters in particular, such rough guidance is generally altogether sufficient. We need not know just how much rain there will be to make it sensible for us to take an umbrella.

Bibliography

Adams, E. W. "Subjective and Indicative Conditionals." *Foundations of Language* 6 (1970): 39–94.

Appiah, Anthony. *Assertion and Conditionals.* Cambridge: Cambridge University Press, 1985.

Aquinas, Thomas. *Summa Theologica.*

Arrow, Kenneth J. "Alternative Approaches to the Theory of Choice in Risk-taking Situations." *Econometrica* 19 (1951): 404–37

Bernoulli, Daniel. "Specimen theoriae novae de mensura sortis" (1730). Translated into German by A. Pringsheim, *Versuch einer neuen Theorie der Wertbestimmung von Glücksfällen.* Leipzig, 1896.

Brandom, Robert. *Making It Explicit.* Cambridge, MA: Harvard University Press, 1994.

Causey, R. L. *Unity of Science.* Dordrecht: Reidel, 1977.

"Common-Sense Reasoning." In *The Routledge Encyclopedia of Philosophy.* London: Routledge, 2000.

Daniels, C. B. "Privacy and Verification." *Analysis* 48 (1988): 100–102.

Davidson, Donald. *Essays on Actions and Events.* New York: Oxford University Press, 1980.

Duhem, Pierre. *The Aim and Structure of Physical Theory.* Translated by P. Wiener. Princeton, NJ: Princeton University Press, 1982.

Dummett, Michael. "Truth." *Proceedings of the Aristotelian Society* 59 (1958–59): 160.

Earman, John. *Bayes or Bust.* Cambridge, MA: MIT Press, 1992.

Eddington, Arthur S. *The Nature of the Physical World.* New York: Macmillan, 1929.

Edgington, Dorothy. "The Paradox of Knowability." *Mind* 94 (1985): 667–68.

Ewing, A. C. *Idealism: A Critical Survey.* London: Methuen, 1934.

Fine, Arthur. "The Natural Ontological Attitude." In *Scientific Realism,* edited by Jarret Lephon. Berkeley: University of California Press, 1984.

Fischoff, Baruch. "Cost-benefit Analysis and the Art of Motorcycle Maintenance." *Policy Sciences* 8 (1977): 177–202.

Fitch, Frederic B. "A Logical Analysis of Some Value Concepts." *Journal of Symbolic Logic* 28 (1963): 135–42.

Green, A. E., and A. J. Bourne. *Reliability Technology*. New York: Wiley-Interscience, 1972.

Harper, William L. "A Sketch of Some Recent Developments in the Theory of Conditionals." In *IFS: Conditionals, Belief, Decision, Chance, and Time*, edited by W. L. Harper, L. G. Pearson, and R. Stalnaker. Dordrecht: D. Reidel, 1981.

Hart, W. D. "The Epistemology of Abstract Objects." *Proceedings of the Aristotelian Society*, 53 (1979, suppl. vol.): 53–65.

Holdren, J. P. "The Nuclear Controversy and the Limitations of Decision Making by Experts." *Bulletin of the Atomic Scientists* 32 (1976): 20–22.

Humberstone, I. L. "The Formalities of Collective Omniscience." *Philosophical Studies* 48 (1985): 401–23.

Jeffrey, Richard C. *The Logic of Decision*, 2nd ed. Chicago, IL: University of Chicago Press, 1983.

Johnson, Frank, ed. *Conditionals*. Oxford: Clarendon Press, 1991.

Kant, Immanuel, *Critique of Pure Reason*.

Kyburg, Henry E. Jr. *Probability and the Logic of Rational Belief*. Middletown, CT: Wesleyan University Press, 1961.

Kyburg, Henry E. Jr., and Chon Man Teng. *Uncertain Inference*. Cambridge: Cambridge University Press, 2001.

Leibniz, G. W. *Philosophische Schriften*, 7 vols. Edited by C. I. Gerhardt. Berlin: Weidmann, 1860–1890.

Lewis, C. I. *An Analysis of Knowledge and Valuation*. La Salle, IL: Open Court, 1962.

Lewis, David. *Conditionals*. Oxford: Blackwell, 1973.

———. "Causal Decision Theory." *Australasian Journal of Philosophy* 59 (1981): 14.

MacIntosh, I. J. "Fitch's Features." *Analysis* 44 (1984): 153–58.

Maimonides. *The Guide for the Perplexed*. Translated by M. Friedlíander. London: Routledge, 1904.

McDowell, John. *Mind and World*. Cambridge, MA: Harvard University Press, 1994; 2nd ed., 1996).

Peirce, Charles S. *Collected Papers of Charles S. Peirce*. Edited by Charles Hartshorne et al. 8 vols. Cambridge, MA: Harvard University Press, 1931–1958.

Plato, *Republic*.

Pollock, J. L. "A Theory of Defeasible Reasoning." *International Journal of Intelligent Systems* 6 (1991): 33–54.

Putnam, Hilary. *Representation and Reality*. Cambridge, MA: Harvard University Press, 1988.

———. *Realism with a Human Face*. Cambridge, MA: Harvard University Press, 1990.

Reid, Thomas. *An Inquiry into the Human Mind*.

————. *Essays on the Intellectual Powers of Man.*

Reiter, Raymond. "Nonmonotonic Reasoning." *Annual Review of Cognitive Science* 2 (1987): 147–86.

Rescher, Nicholas. "Belief-contravening Suppositions." *Philosophical Review* 70 (1961): 176–196.

————. *Hypothetical Reasoning.* Amsterdam: North Holland, 1964.

————. *Methodological Pragmatism.* Oxford: Basil Blackwell, 1977.

————. *Scientific Progress.* Oxford: Basil Blackwell, 1978.

————. *Induction.* Oxford: Blackwell, 1980.

————. *Empirical Inquiry.* Totowa, NJ: Rowman & Littlefield, 1982.

————. *Risk.* Lanham, MD: University Press of America, 1983.

————. *The Limits of Science.* Berkeley: University of California Press, 1984.

————. *The Strife of Systems.* Pittsburgh, PA: University of Pittsburgh Press, 1985.

————. *Scientific Realism.* Dordrecht: D. Reidel, 1987.

————. *Rationality.* Oxford: Oxford University Press, 1988.

————. *Cognitive Economy.* Pittsburgh, PA: University of Pittsburgh Press, 1989.

————. *A Useful Inheritance.* Savage, MD: Rowman & Littlefield, 1990.

————. *Philosophical Standardism.* Pittsburgh, PA: University of Pittsburgh Press, 1994.

————. *Satisfying Reason.* Dordrecht: Kluwer, 1995.

————. *Priceless Knowledge?* Lanham, MD: University Press of America, 1996.

————. *Predicting the Future.* Albany, NY: SUNY Press, 1997.

————. *Realistic Pragmatism.* Albany, NY: SUNY Press, 2000.

————. *Nature and Understanding.* Oxford: Clarendon Press, 2002.

Rorty, Richard. *Consequences of Pragmatism.* Minneapolis, MN: University of Minnesota Press, 1982.

Ross, W. D. *Aristotle's Prime and Posterior Analytics.* Oxford: Clarendon Press, 1949.

Routley, Richard. "Necessary Limits to Knowledge: Unknown Truths." In *Essays in Scientific Philosophy,* edited by E. Morscher et al., 93–113. Bad Reichenhall: Comes, 1981.

Russell, Bertrand. *Human Knowledge: Its Scope and Limits.* Simon & Schuster, 1948.

Salmon, Wesley C. *Four Decades of Scientific Explanation.* Minneapolis, MN: University of Minnesota Press, 1989.

Simon, Herbert A. *The Sciences of the Artificial.* Cambridge, MA: MIT Press, 1969. 2nd ed., 1981.

Slote, Michael A. *Beyond Optimizing.* Cambridge, MA: Harvard University Press, 1989.

Slovic, Paul. "Behavioral Decision Theory." *Annual Review of Psychology* 28 (1977): 1–39.

Slovic, Paul, et al. "Preference for Insuring Against Probable Small Losses: Insurance Implications." *Journal of Risk and Insurance* 44 (1977): 237–258.

Sorensen, Roy A. *Blindspots.* Oxford: Clarendon Press, 1988.

Sosa, Ernest, ed. *Causation and Conditionals.* London: Oxford University Press, 1975.

Tversky, Amos, and D. Kahneman, "Judgment Under Uncertainty: Heuristics and Biases." *Science* 185 (1974): 1124–31.

Vollmer, Gerhard. *Wissenschaftstheorie am Einsatz.* Stuttgart: Hirzel, 1993.

Wigner, E. P. "The Limits of Science." *Proceedings of the American Philosophical Society* 93 (1949): 521–26.

———. "The Unreasonable Effectiveness of Mathematics in the Natural Sciences." *Communications on Pure and Applied Mathematics* 13 (1960): 1–14.

Williamson, Timothy, "Intuitionism Disproved?" *Analysis* 42 (1982): 203–207.

———. "On Knowledge of the Unknowable." *Analysis* 47 (1987): 154–58.

———. "On the Paradox of Knowability." *Mind* 96 (1987): 256–61.

———. "Knowability and Constructivism." *Philosophical Quarterly* 38 (1988): 422–43.

———. "On Intuitionistic Modal Epistemic Logic." *Journal of Philosophical Logic* 21 (1992): 63–89.

———. *Knowledge and Its Limits.* Oxford: Oxford University Press, 2000.

Zemach, E. M. "Are There Logical Limits for Science?" *British Journal for the Philosophy of Science* 38 (1987): 527–32.

Index